Julian Chitta

GUN CONTROL

A CONTRADICTION IN TERMS

Copyright © 2018 by Julian Chitta. All Rights Reserved.

CONTENTS

Introduction	3	Points to Ponder	78
Firearm owner Protection	14	Anatomy of a Home Invasion	82
Concealed Carry	21	Women and Guns	89
Open Carry	32	Children and Guns	94
Anatomy of a Bank Robbery	38	Christianity and Guns	100
Anatomy of a Massacre	46	Islamism and Guns	102
Resisting Criminal Attacks	55	Crime Control	106
Fatal Gun Attraction	60	Stopping Gun Violence	110
Surviving a Home invasion	62	Gun Safety	116
Anatomy of a Carjacking	67	Gun Running	119
Crime Politics	71	Surviving an Active Shooter	124
Stopping the Gun Violence	75	Epilogue	127

INTRODUCTION

The term "Gun Control" should refer strictly to one's ability to hit a target, however, the intervention of the legal profession confers to the same notion, a much more contorted meaning, as a vast collection of laws and regulations meant to short-circuit the constitutional guarantees. The intervention of lawyers resulted, in absolutely every state, in a myriad of laws and regulations intended to limit civilians' access to firearms. That encompasses all the aspects connected to this industry, in regard to the manufacture of firearms, from sale, transfer, possession, and use elements.

The proponents of absolute gun control argue that the widespread gun ownership somehow degrades the quality of life in the USA, by an increase in crime, homicides and suicides. The statistics do not support such a hypothesis.

The opponents to the gun control demonstrate, quite successfully, that the possession of firearms reduces crime and does not increase gun-injuries or suicides. Their statistical data, compiled by law enforcement agencies, demonstrates unequivocally that law-abiding gun owners are much better at preventing crime, than the state or federal bureaucrats, determining many criminal elements to move away from the areas where the local citizenry possesses firearms. Aside from the constitutional considerations based on the Second Amendment to the US Constitution, the idea of limiting personal liberty through laws and regulations, without the consent of the people, does not gain any kind of significant sympathy for the gun control advocates.

The Marxist-inspired drive to outlaw all small arms, pistols, rifles and shotguns, has experienced a strong resistance. Most of the criteria artificially selected, were intended to classify repeating rifles and semi-automatic pistols as "assault weapons", to fall in line with specific UN proposals for world-wide interdiction of civilian gun ownership.

By analyzing the data furnished by the UN's Economic and Social Council, (1991), in dealing with firearm issues, one can easily came to the conclusion that the entire UN action is meant to single out the United States of America and Yemen, as the two countries which do not make any effort to limit civilian firearm ownership. According to the same source, the USA civilian population accounts for some 310 million small firearms, out of which some 27 million units are in the hands of civilian law enforcement agencies, while the rest of the world can claim about 995 million units, for both, civilian and military use.

Criminal gangs and drug cartels are estimated to possess and use more than 10 million firearms. (One can legitimately question the data published and its validity. How can you assess the number of weapons in the hands of the secretive criminals?)The "imported" criminal gangs, like MS-13 and others complicated these assessments even more.

In 1997 the UN published several studies regarding small arms and local regulations. Such a study, titled the United Nations International Study on Firearm Regulations, finished in 1999, proposed the initiation of a world-wide effort to establish a database for all civilian firearms, in order to make the Center for International Crime Prevention, in Vienna, a clearing house for monitoring all the small arms movement. This UN division was charged with the civilian firearms regulation coordination, with the expressed goal of banning all civilian firearms. The conclusions of the biennial reviews were supposed to be imposed upon all UN member countries, however, the opposition from Muslim countries and from the USA, made it impossible for the UN to come with any coherent plan of action, placing that issue on a back burner for the next two decades, in the hope of being able to reactivate it.

In response to the UN proposals, the US ambassador to UN, John Bolton, insisted that the US Constitution needs to supersede any accords and conventions not ratified by the US Congress, thus the UN removed most all paragraphs of the 2001 UN Program of Action on Small Arms, in which the idea of banning all civilian arms is spelled out in detail. In spite of the efforts of the US Secretaries of State, John Kerry and Hillary Clinton, to revive the UN initiative on banning civilian firearms, and attempts to get a specific legislative action in, through the back door, by determining the USA President to issue illegal executive orders. The US Congress never debated that issue, even if the senate majority leader, at that time, Harry Reid, tried to force on, his leftist initiatives, as did the past Speaker of the House, Nancy Pelosi.

Noteworthy at this point, is the stance taken by the Nevada senator, Harry Reid, who, being in the middle of his electoral campaign, changed his position, becoming a gun rights fan. (Nevada is a state in which firearm ownership is widely distributed among city and rural dwellers alike.)

The process of aligning the USA laws with the UN requirements for the total control of the civilian firearms was thus dead on arrival.

Historically, the gun ownership politics did not enter the arena of the hot public debates until late 1920s and early 1930s, when the mobs of the larger cities, like New York, Chicago, and Philadelphia, engaged in bloody wars, which claimed victims among innocent civilians. The media and the public did demand measures that fanned the appetite for gun control among some of the politicians. As a result, the large cities, under a concentrated effort from the part of several federal specialized law enforcement agencies, tried to stop the proliferation of firearms in the hands of the criminals, unsuccessfully. Consequently, the public opinion was soon split between those who supported, and those who opposed gun control laws, but this issue never reached any significant intensity until the early 1990s.

The debates about firearm availability, and the issue of gun violence, reached a boiling point, when the concerns for personal liberties, such as the right to bear arms, as specified in the amendments to the US Constitution, specifically the Second Amendment, became "hot potatoes" which few of the politicians would dare to touch.

The split between some gun control advocates, and the supporters of the traditional American individual rights, both with some valid logical points of view, continues to this day to dominate the discussions, where finding a common ground seem impossible.

The government mission of serving the needs of the people, by preventing crime and deaths, is severely impeded by archaic laws which place more importance on the rights of the criminals, than on the rights of the law-abiding citizens. Gun control supporters sustain that the unrestricted firearm ownership inhibits the government from fulfilling its precise constitutional responsibilities.

The gun rights supporters promote firearm ownership for several reasons, which all have to do with the citizenry's ability to prevent any kind of tyranny, promoting security. Self-defense, hunting, and sport shooting, are legitimate reasons to own and use firearms, yet most of the leftists look with disdain upon such an American tradition.

If you consider the origination points of this toxic drive to deprive law-abiding citizens of certain constitutionally-protected rights, you will find that most of the authors of the requests to totally ban firearms in civilian hands come from people who are usually immigrants, with an anti-American agenda, foreigners, or UN bureaucrats.

George Soros, the hedge-fund billionaire, finances up to this day, hundreds of "anti-gun" organizations, to the tune of some 100 million per year, in spite of major setbacks in the recent elections, in which he supported only left candidates, including Barack Hussein Obama II, and Hillary Clinton.

The "anti-gun lobby" is extremely powerful, reaching into the heart of all US economic sectors, from finance to agriculture. Several US gun manufacturers and dealers had to close shop, or to relocate to other states, because some of the major banks "did not like to deal with them".

Historically, several attempts to limit all the firearm ownership aspects, at federal level, have been proposed and eventually tabled off by the US Congress, few times.

The National Firearms Act of 1934 was conceived to offer some solutions to the problem of acute mob violence, achieving only questionable success. That Act, under its Title II, prohibits the interstate transfer and transport for certain classes of weapons, primarily of "sub-machinegun type", like the well-known Thompsons and Colt military issues. The Bureau of Alcohol, Tobacco, and Firearms, the BATF, was thus charged with the administration of any and all aspects of enforcement, yet the gangsters continued to use the same unregistered weapons, without paying any of the excise taxes imposed by that Act. Through the clauses spelled out in the National Firearms Act, NFA, of 1934, the federal agencies could ban any weapon, rifle or shotgun, with a barrel shorter than 14", and 16" later, on the assumption that this way only the criminal element would use such firearms. The pistols and the revolvers were not affected.

The National Firearms Act of 1934 described in detail all the types of weapons and accessories covered by its four prohibiting clauses:

- Machine guns, or weapons which can fire more than one round on a single trigger pull;

- Short-barreled rifles, or rifles, with a butt stock and a barrel shorter than 16";

- Short-barreled shotguns, with a barrel shorter than 18";

- Suppressors or silencers, the devices used to muffle the sound of gunfire.

In spite of the efforts of the federal agencies to control the violence connected to firearms, the 1934 Act had minimal impact on the criminal gang activities.

In 1968, at the urging of the then US president, Lyndon Baines Johnson, the Congress passed the Gun Control Act of 1968, which practically stopped all the movement of firearms through the interstate commerce, except under the protection of the licenses of manufacturers and importers, banning any mail-order sales of firearms. The motivation for passing of this act was provided to the USA Congress, in the aftermath of the assassinations of John F, Kennedy, Martin Luther King, Jr., and Robert F. Kennedy.

President John F. Kennedy was allegedly shot with a mail-order rifle purchased by the assassin from the catalogue of the National Rifle Association's magazine, the "American Rifleman".

At the congressional hearings, where the ban on all mail order sales of firearms was discussed, the NRA executive vice-president at that time, Franklin Orth, declared quite unequivocally that his organization supports fully such an act:

"We do not think that any sane American could object to any bill which will offer the instrument to prevent the assassination of any public figure."

The Act defines precisely some categories of people who were prohibited from acquiring firearms, in 18 U.S.C. 922 (c), such as felons, mentally ill people, drug addicts, gang members, foreign citizens, and vagrants.

This Act provided realistic measures to safeguard our civil rights about the possession and use of firearms by ordinary citizens, yet the bureaucrats charged with the implementation of the Gun Control Act of 1968, soon will find ways to sabotage the Congressional intent.

Consequently, it was increasingly difficult to obtain a dealer Federal Firearm License, or one for a gunsmith. The same Act prohibits the direct mail ordering of firearms, but it allows for shipments of firearms by US Mail, UPS, FedEx, etc. to a gun-smith, (who needs to have a Federal Firearm License), or to the gun manufacturer, for repairs. After the

the firearm's repair, the gunsmith or the factory service department, may ship the firearm back to the original customer.

The only problems encountered along the lines of working to track weapons used in crime, are offered by the lack of sufficient specialists to fulfill this role. Slow response and inaccurate data still plagues the fight for justice against the habitual criminals.

As a side note, please observe that for decades, after the passing of the Gun Control Act of 1968, no one mentioned mass killings in schools, universities, or in child care centers. It seems that the gun violence took a new turn toward the innocent members of our society, least prepared to survive such barbarism. Most all perpetrators of those despicable acts were people who shouldn't have had access to firearms, since they were felons, mentally ill, drug addicts, and no exigency of that law could have prevented such tragedies. The saying that:

"When faced by a bad guy with a gun, it is infinitely better to have a good guy with a gun, on your side",

rings very true for most everyone, even if many institutions advertise that "This is a gun-free zone", giving the bad guys the assurances they need to do their abject deeds, confident that no one would shoot back at them, before the law people arrive.

Are you still against owning a gun?

The ownership of a firearm implies a tremendous level of responsibility, which may start with answering a few questions:

1. Are you confident enough in properly handling a gun? (If not, get all the training necessary.)

2. Would you know exactly when to use your weapon and when not? (Again, get proper training and practice.)

3. Are you observant enough, to recall all the details, in a crime scene, so that you can help the police?

Keep in mind at all times, that your gun is only an inanimate object, and that guns do not kill people. Only people kill people. And the term "people" includes toddlers, young children, and adolescents, who do not need to have access to firearms. Guns may put their parents into a situation of extreme liability, if their minor children get hold of those guns. The firearms in a household do need to be properly stored, so that no accidents due to parental negligence can happen. The youngest shooter ever recorded was a five-years-old boy who killed his three-years-old sister, with his father's handgun he pulled out of a night stand drawer. As tragic as that event was, the child could not be considered as having any culpability, for being too young to be considered at the age of reason.

In the American jurisprudence only the children older than 12-years of age are regarded as of reason age.

That's why anyone living in a household with small children has to devise a way to keep firearms safely out of the reach of children. There are a lot of publications and materials that can provide the needed information to do that, among which the NRA-originated magazines and books can provide all the necessary data.

Contrary to popular opinions fanned in the mass media, the ownership of a firearm is a right, not a privilege. Some of the citizens would lose their rights, following the commission of felonies. That goes also for voting rights and the eligibility to apply for certain state or federal jobs.

The deportment during military service will influence seriously, also, availability of certain rights. An individual discharged dishonorably from the military service, loses also the right to own and use firearms. That's not a retributive measure, but a safety-dictated option for the state.

FIREARM OWNERS' PROTECTION

The Firearms Owners' Protection Act, passed in 1986 by a Republican majority in both chambers of the Congress, is a federal law meant to revise the Gun Control Act of 1968, on the basis of a more user-friendly, streamlined approach.

In the past, according to critics, the Bureau of Alcohol, Tobacco and Firearms, did not discharge its responsibilities in consistent manner, selecting to execute a selective enforcement of the law, on the assumption that it is infinitely easier to deal with law-abiding legal firearm owners, who do not shot at you, than to enforce the law against felons, gangsters, and drug cartel members.

Consequently, the numerous complaints against ATF abuses did reach the US Congress, and the NRA, became the leader in requesting added legal scrutiny. The Senate committee charged with overseeing the ATF work, convened in the February 1982 hearings, concluding that certain administrative measures imposed by the Gun Control Act of 1968 were too arbitrary. Please note the text on page 179:

"This conclusion is thus inescapable, that the history, the words, and the spirit of the Second Amendment to the Constitution of the USA, as well as its interpretation by many scholars or the Federal Courts during the first century after its ratification in 1791, indicates that what is protected, is the individual right of a private citizen to carry firearms peacefully."

During its investigations that followed, the same subcommittee found that over 75 % of the ATF prosecutions were based on evidence "fabricated" by some federal agents, who aimed "to nail ordinary citizens", who had no criminal intent or knowledge, but "were enticed, with money, by the ATF agents", to do the things that they normally would not do.

The Congress put an end to that arbitrary practice. Moreover, the new law came with several ground-breaking provisions, in the Firearm Owners' Protection Act, by asserting that a violator of the law cannot be considered guilty of anything, until pronounced as such by a court at law, and placed the issues of enforcement, in synchronization with rest of the articles of the US Constitution.

Some of the items, that can be considered new, protect well the firearms owners, even outside their normal residential area:

1. The Right to safe passage through other jurisdictions. In the past, law enforcement agencies randomly searched out of state vehicles and confiscated any firearms found in them, laying heavy fines on the unfortunate souls who just happened to pass through. Thus, a person who travels from one place to another cannot be incarcerated for a firearm offense, in a state that has stricter gun control laws, if the traveler is just passing through. Short stops for rest, food or fuel, do not count in this sense. The deciding factor in ascertaining such a situation is based on the fact that the firearm shall be unloaded and not to be readily available to the driver, while any ammunition has to be stored separately, preferably in a locked up container. What consists in a "loaded gun", a round in the chamber, an empty clip, a full clip?

Under such a scenario, a citizen resident of Virginia cannot be arrested for traveling through New Jersey, or New York, for possessing a handgun, provided that this same individual did not stop in New Jersey or New York, for an extended period of time. 18 USC 926 A does not specify exactly what an "extended period of time" is. One hour, six, overnight?

2. The Prohibition Against Firearms Registration, decreed in this Act is being short-circuited regularly, by the ATF and other federal or state agencies, which all maintain huge data bases with the particulars of the owner, the brand of firearm, and its serial number, in spite of clear instructions to the contrary, advanced by the US Attorney General:

"No such rule or regulation, prescribed by the office of the United States Attorney General, after the date of the enactment of this Firearms Owners' Protection Act, may not require that records may be maintained under this chapter, or any portions thereof, in order to be created, recorded, or also transferred to any facility owned, managed or controlled by the USA, or any State, or any political subdivision thereof, not that nor any system of registration of firearms, firearms owners, or firearms transactions, or their dispositions may be established. Nothing in this particular section of this law restricts or expands, the Secretary's authority to inquire into the acts of firearm transfers, in the course of any criminal investigations."

Nevertheless, the contradiction in terms provided by the recent practices of the Obama administration, point quite well to the ATF's data bases which track all the gun owners through the

- Firearm Tracking System, the FTS, to the tune of over 200 million gun owners, and data obtained from qualified sales, with accent on specific transactions:

- Multiple Sales Reports. In 2012 over 5.5 million gun transaction were qualified as "multiple sales", when one individual purchased more than one gun. The spur in gun sales can be traced directly to the Obama administration's aversion for armed citizens.

- Suspected Gun Lists. Such recordkeeping elements are designed to intercept transactions in which firearms purchased legally have been used in the commission of certain crimes. The estimated number of such firearms was at a level of approximately 69,000 in 2015.

- Traced Guns Lists. This database contains quite a large number of firearms, owners, and guns, along the entire physical life of the targeted elements, from initial manufacture, to the retail sale, to the final disposition, other than a transfer through sale, with the name of the selling dealer, and that of the purchaser clearly recorded. The total was approximately 5.5 million units in 2015.

- Stolen-Gun Lists. All the firearms reported as stolen, from local dealers, and or from interstate carriers, are all combined on such a list. The ATF does not maintain an interface with FBI's National Crime Information Center, the NCIC, where most of the stolen, missing, or lost firearms are listed as a permanent record. This database had approximately 45,000 entries in 2015.

- Out of Business Gun Dealers. This vital statistical data is compiled by tabulating all the ATF Forms 4473, which advise the agency about the closing of gun dealerships, but do not specify the reasons. In 2012 alone approximately 14,000 dealerships, and 980 gunsmith shops closed their doors.

Following the assassination attempt on President Ronald Reagan, the Congress passed in 1993 the Brady Handgun Violence Prevention Act, which mandated the establishment of a specific federal investigative instrument, capable to weed out any would-be firearm buyers, who are prohibited by law from obtaining them. A waiting period was established, with mandatory background checks intended to focus on persons who may pose a serious threat to public safety, and to themselves. The records obtained through the background checks, are to be destroyed, after 24 hours. Many times, an individual barred from buying a firearm, may fall through the system's checks, because of this short 24 hour retention period, and the inability of the computers used to properly communicate with each other. In spite of elaborate and expansive attempts to prevent, any "prohibited persons", from obtaining firearms, over 50 % of the cases in which recently purchased firearms, were used to commit horrible crimes, could be traced to this flaw in the system. The federal government and its agencies cannot effectively try to prevent the proliferation of firearms into the hands of the criminals, even with the use of an extremely elaborate and extensive list of "prohibited persons":

- Felons convicted to more than one year in prison;

- Fugitives from justice;

- Drug addicts and abusers of alcohol or controlled substances;

- Anyone adjudicated as a mentally deficient person, or has been involuntarily institutionalized in a mental hospital;

- Illegal aliens;

- Persons discharged from military service other than honorably;

- Anyone who has renounced his US citizenship;

- Anyone recently convicted of a misdemeanor crime of domestic violence;

- Persons who are under information or indictment, for any crimes which could result in a detention period of over two years;

In spite of its huge size, somehow, this data base fails frequently to single out the people who later are found to be the perpetrators of unspeakable acts of murder, in school zones, or where no one would expect that, like in the case of the Baptist Church of Sutherland Springs, Texas, where, the

26-years-old Devin Patrick Kelley murdered 26, and injured 20 other people.

Kelley was prohibited by law from purchasing or possessing any firearms and ammunition due to several domestic violence convictions in a court-martial while in the US Air Force. The Air Force failed to record the convictions, in the FBI's National Crime Information Center database, which is used in the National Instant Check System to flag prohibited purchasers. The error prompted the Air Force to begin a review of its procedures regarding the process of reporting felonies committed by its personnel.

That attack was the deadliest mass shooting by one person in Texas, and the fourth-deadliest mass shooting in a US place of worship, next to the 2015 Charleston church shooting in which 33 people were killed, or the 1991 Waddell Buddhist temple massacre, in which 9 monks of Thai descent were murdered.

The common denominator in all those massacres was the fact that all the shooters involved should have been prohibited from acquire firearms, if the National Crime Info Center of the FBI would have been properly updated.

That type of failure raises serious questions about the methods used by the law enforcement agencies, which, some of the times fail to follow the federal law. That raises the issue of the promulgation of new gun control laws, while those laws already existing are not enforced.

CONCEALED CARRY

The concealed carry, or carrying a concealed weapon, CCW, is the practice of carrying a weapon (such as a handgun) in public in a concealed manner, on one's person or in close proximity. Not all weapons that fall under CCW laws are lethal. For example, in Florida, carrying pepper spray in more than a specified volume (2 oz.) of chemical requires a CCW permit, whereas anyone may legally carry a smaller, "self-defense chemical spray" device hidden on their person without a CCW permit. As of 2017 there have been 16.3 million concealed weapon permits issued in the United States.

There is no federal statute concerning the issuance of the concealed-carry permits. All fifty stated have passed laws allowing qualified individuals to carry certain concealed firearms in public, either without a permit or after obtaining a permit from a specific government authority at the state and/or local level.

A comprehensive 2014 study by the National Academy of Science concluded that there was no evidence that concealed carry either increases or reduces violent crime; some individual studies suggest that CCW reduces violent crime; others suggest that it increases violent crime. In any case, the criminals who may expect that some potential victims carry handguns renounce to commit violent crimes. That is a significant difference between the states which grant

CCW permits relatively easily, and those states that have prohibitive rules, like Illinois, New York, Maryland or DC.

Regulations differ widely from state to state, with most states currently maintaining a "May Issue" policy. As recently as 1980, to 1990, most states were "No Issue" jurisdictions, but over the past 20 years the same states have consistently moved to less restrictive alternatives.

There is currently a split between several federal circuit courts regarding the standards for issuance of permits and the right to carry weapons outside the home. The 9th and 3rd circuits have ruled in favor of inflexible permitting policies, while the 7th and D.C. circuits have ruled that the states are not required to try to force stricter policies, because the right to carry weapons extends outside the home.

The Federal Gun Free School Zones Act limits where any unlicensed person may carry a gun, openly or concealed, within 1,000 feet (300 m) of a school zone is prohibited, with exceptions granted in the Federal law to holders of valid State-issued weapons permits while state laws may reassert the illegality of school zone carry by license holders, under current laws retired policemen and other law enforcement officers regardless of permit are exempt from such limitations.

When in contact with an officer, some states require that a CCW holder informs that officer that person is carrying a handgun. For detailed information on the individual states' permitting rules one shall address the states' Departments of Public Safety.

In the United States of America, all concealed carry permits are recognized in reciprocity, except for California, Connecticut, District of Columbia, Guam, Hawaii, Maryland, Massachusetts, New Jersey, New York, and Oregon. The US Congress is debating the possibility to legislate reciprocity for all CCW permits within the US territory.

In unrestricted jurisdictions, in which a CCW is not required based on the Second Amendment provisions, thus those states are called constitutional carry states. Within the unrestricted category, there may be some states that are fully unrestricted, where no permit is required for lawful open or concealed carry. In other unrestricted jurisdictions some forms of carry may require a permit.

Among U.S. states, Alaska, Arizona, Arkansas, Idaho, (residents only), Kansas, Maine, Mississippi, Missouri, New Hampshire, North Dakota (residents only; concealed carry only), Vermont, West Virginia, and Wyoming, (residents only), are fully unrestricted, and allow those who are not prohibited from owning a firearm to carry a concealed firearm in any place not deemed off-limits by law without a permit. Idaho, North Dakota and Wyoming only extend open carry only to residents of the state; non-residents must still have a permit issued by their home state to legally carry concealed in these states. Concealed carry in Mississippi, only covers certain manners of carrying. These states also allow the open carry of a handgun without a permit with the exception of North Dakota and within certain counties in Missouri.

Certain states, like Montana, New Mexico, and Oklahoma are in partially unrestricted jurisdictions. Specifically, Montana would currently allow concealed carry without a permit in places outside of any incorporated municipalities. New Mexico laws allow any individual to conceal carry an unloaded handgun without a permit. New Mexico further allows one to carry a loaded handgun either openly or concealed while traveling in a vehicle, including on a motorcycle, recreational vehicles (RV), bicycle, or while riding a horse. Oklahoma allows residents of other states' citizens to carry openly or concealed guns without a permit, provided that any such people have valid IDs from their home state. All in the list of the aforementioned states will recognize all permits to carry issued by other states.

In recent cases challenging restrictive discretionary issue laws, federal district and appeals courts have generally applied the intermediate scrutiny thesis.

The intermediate scrutiny thesis, in the American constitutional law, is the second level of deciding issues using the judicial review for adjudication. The other levels are typically referred to as the reviews on a rational basis, (least rigorous), and the strict scrutiny, (most rigorous).

In order to overcome the intermediate scrutiny test, it must be shown that the law or policy being challenged only furthers an important government interest, by means that are substantially related to that interest. That should be contrasted with the strict scrutiny, the higher standard of review that requires a narrowly tailored, and the least restrictive means to further a compelling governmental interest, not otherwise specifically stated in statute. The constitutional Equal Protection analysis applies not only to challenges against the federal government, but also against the state and local governments.

Although the Fourteenth Amendment's Equal Protection Clause applies only to state and local governments, the United States Supreme Court has implied an Equal Protection limitation on the federal government through a process known as a primary thesis of "reversed interpretation". As the Fourteenth Amendment applies directly to the states, the incorporation process was not necessary to hold this restriction against state and local authorities. Equal Protection analysis also applies to both legislative and executive actions regardless if the actions are of a substantive or procedural nature. Judicially crafted rules that follow common law, are also valid only if they conform to the requirements of Equal Protection.

Most states require concealed carry applicants to certify their proficiency with a firearm through some type of specific training or instruction. Certain training courses developed by the NRA that combine classroom and live-fire instruction, typically meet most state training requirements. Some states recognize prior military or police service as meeting training requirements.

Classroom instruction would typically include gun mechanics and terminology, cleaning and maintenance of a firearm concealed carry legislation and limitations, liability issues, carry methods and safety, home defense, methods for managing and defusing any confrontational situations, and practice of gun handling techniques without firing the weapon. Most required CCW training courses devote a considerable amount of time to liability issues.

Depending on the state, a practical component during which the attendee shoots the weapon for the purpose of demonstrating safety and proficiency may be required.

During range instruction, applicants would typically learn and demonstrate safe handling and operation of a firearm for accurate shooting from a common self-defense distance. Some states require a certain level of proficiency in order to receive a passing grade, whereas other states (e.g., Florida) technically require only a single-shot be fired to demonstrate handgun handling proficiency.

Many jurisdictions recognize a permit or license issued by other jurisdictions. Recognition may be granted to all jurisdictions or some subset which meets a group of permit-issuing criteria, such as training comparable to that used in the original jurisdiction, or certain background checks. Several states have entered into mutual agreements to recognize such permits. This arrangement is commonly called reciprocity or mutual recognition. A few states do not recognize permits issued by any other jurisdiction, but offer non-resident permits for out-of-state individuals (who possess a valid concealed carry permit from their home state), who wish to carry while visiting such states. There are also states that neither recognize out-of-state concealed carry permits nor issue permits to non-residents, resulting into a complete ban on concealed carry by non-residents.

While generally a concealed carry permit allows the permit holder to carry a concealed weapon in public, a state may restrict carry of a firearm including a permitted concealed weapon while in or on certain properties, facilities, or types of businesses that are otherwise open to the public. These areas vary by state (except for the first item below: Federal facilities or public offices are subject to superseding Federal law) and may extend to:

Federal government facilities, including post offices, IRS offices, federal court buildings, military/VA facilities, and/or correctional facilities, Amtrak trains and facilities, and Corps of Engineers-controlled property;

State and local facilities, including courthouses, DMV or DoT offices, police stations, correctional facilities, and or meeting places of government entities (exceptions may be made for certain persons working in these facilities such as judges, lawyers, and certain government officials both elected or appointed)

Venues for political events, including any rallies, parades, polling places, and political candidate conferences.

Educational institutions, like schools, colleges, universities.

Amusement parks, fairs, parades, and carnivals.

Businesses that sell alcohol.

Hospitals.

Churches.

Airports.

Aboard airplanes, or ships.

Onboard public transportation trains, or vehicles.

Any private property, that banns guns.

Non-government critical facilities, such as some large nuclear laboratories, power plants, dams, oil, gas, production plants, banks, or other types of businesses that display certain announcements at the entrance, prohibiting firearms.

The issue of liability for CCW permits is quite complex. Even when self-defense is justified, there can be serious civil or criminal liabilities related to self-defense, when a concealed carry permit holder brandishes or fires his or her weapon. For example, if innocent bystanders are hurt or killed, there could be both civil and criminal liabilities, even if the use of deadly force was completely justified. Some states technically allow an assailant who is shot by a gun owner to bring civil action. In some states, liability is present when a resident brandishes the weapon, threatens use, or escalates or exacerbates a volatile situation, or when the resident is carrying while intoxicated. It is important to note that simply pointing a firearm at any person constitutes a felony assault with a deadly weapon, unless circumstances validate the need to use deadly force. A majority of states who allow concealed carry, however, forbid civil suits being brought in such cases, either by barring lawsuits for damages resulting from a criminal act on the part of the plaintiff, or by granting the gun owner immunity from such a civil suit if it is found that he or she was justified in shooting.

The increased number of states, which passed into law the "Castle Doctrine" concept, allows persons who own firearms and or carry them concealed, to use them without first attempting to retreat, removing the liability issue.

Illustrative in this sense are the numerous cases of home invasions in which the perpetrators have been shot dead. Repeatedly the courts have found such cases as bona fide self-defense, and no charges were ever filed against the homeowners who did not retreat and defended their "castle".

Most all the cases in which the criminals' families did start civil proceedings to claim damages caused by the death of the home invader(s) have been dismissed, and the most all appeals to the higher courts have been rejected.

Following the extension of the "castle doctrine", several states enacted new laws, for more effective prosecution in the circumstances of home invasion, extending that reasoning to mobile homes, motorhomes, boat homes, and to tents, with the very few exceptions in Illinois, New York and Maryland, states in which the criminal element seems to be better protected, than the law-abiding citizens. It is impossible not to notice that the states that limit arbitrarily the issuance of concealed carry, have the highest crime rates. That fact will invalidate the official position that the criminals would respect the new laws limiting firearm ownership.

The fact that two states, New Jersey and New York do not consider manslaughter in self-defense as a legitimate standing in a court at law, explains why violent assaults in those states increased their number five fold. Those acts are primarily described as armed muggings of people carrying concealed weapons, while in transit. In one particular case, the mugger attacked an out of state driver while filling up his vehicle. The criminal pointed a gun at the driver demanding his billfold. The driver removed the pump nuzzle from the car thank and drenched the mugger with gasoline. The mugger fired a shot, hitting his victim in the shoulder. The driver returned fire killing the criminal. The ensuing fire caused over two million dollars in damages to the filling station. The driver was hospitalized for five days, after which he was imprisoned for manslaughter. It took him three months to get out on bail, and finally to have his case dismissed. That cost him over $50,000.

His law suit against the filling station, which failed to insure the safety of its customers, was dismissed on the basis that the particular area of that city was a high-crime area, and the customers should have known that.

What that example did illustrate was the fact that an individual permitted to carry a concealed weapon, should be thoroughly familiar with the elements that warrant the use of deadly force, and not to do it. The bandit at the filling station was punished enough by setting himself ablaze, when he fired his gun. He would have died anyway, since no one tried to put the fire out, while the victim would have been better off by just resigning to the situation. Most likely he fired in anger, when he killed the mugger, and, at the same time, he performed a charitable act by stopping the suffering of that man dying burned alive.

If you can, avoid pulling your gun. If you do it, make sure that you know exactly where you want your bullet to hit, before you have your gun in hand.

Conflict de-escalation shall be a technique that all CCW people shall master, yet there are very few programs that can train you psychologically on how to avoid an all-out fight.

The oriental "peaceful warriors" have got it right.

OPEN CARRY

In all states, the commonwealths, and the territories of the United States, the US Constitution is the fundamental law and all its amendments are fully applicable equally, including the Second Amendment, in regard to the right of the citizenry to own and carry firearms.

Regardless of the technicalities involved in some facts in related the act of owning, using, and carrying firearms, there are only two situations, which warrant a second look at the most prevalent situations:

1. Concealed carry of personal weapons, under which any lawfully permitted person can carry, usually means a gun not easily discernible by a casual observer. Compare this statement with the "legal definition" of a concealed gun, as stated in several jurisdictions – like in Oklahoma, Texas, Utah, Montana, Ohio, or Missouri – with a minimal of differences in other states:

"Concealed handgun" means a handgun with a presence that is not openly discernible to the ordinary observation of a reasonable person. In most states, however, in order to carry a concealed gun, a person shall possess a proper state license.

To obtain such a license, an applicant has to fill a form, which usually requires a photograph of the applicant, copy of the applicant's birth certificate, proof of state residency, a full set of fingerprints, evidence of handgun proficiency as proof of an approved course, and an authorization, from a specific state subdivision, for a current investigation into the current applicant's background, and criminal history records. Some states may require also, a medical examination. At any rate, all permits to carry a concealed handgun have limited validity and shall be renewed periodically.

Only the following states, commonwealths, and US territories have the legal means in place to grant concealed handgun licenses, as January 2018:

Arkansas, Connecticut, Georgia, Guam, Hawaii, Indiana, Iowa, Maryland, Massachusetts, Minnesota, Missouri, New Jersey, North Dakota, Oklahoma, Rhode Island, Tennessee, Texas and Utah.

2. Open carry of personal weapons, refers to the practice of openly carrying firearms in public. Even though many authorities confirm that this custom is a throw-back from the days of the Wild West, the current resurgence in "open carry" is no surprise, in view of the fact that criminal activities spread out from Mexico into the large cities, and threaten rural America, the only place that can offer the resistance needed to overcome the wave of lawlessness that comes down from Chicago, New York, Baltimore or Miami.

The interpretation of the notion of "open carry" varies from state to state, yet the meaning is uniform: a handgun in plain sight, of any one regardless various semantic angles.

Certain states like a handgun "partially visible" or "fully visible". The states which have open carry provisions are:

Alabama, Alaska, Arizona, Colorado, Delaware, Idaho, Kansas, Kentucky, Louisiana, Maine, Michigan, Mississippi, Montana, Nevada, New Mexico, North Carolina, Ohio, South Dakota, Texas, (as of 1/1/2017), Vermont, Virginia, Washington, West Virginia, Wisconsin and Wyoming.

The realization that certain states, extremely unfriendly to the armed law-abiding citizens, like Illinois, New York and Maryland, are emblematic of the mind set of their feeble legislators, who value much more the lives of the perpetrators of crime, than that of their tax payers, causing the massive population moves toward Texas, Oklahoma, Washington and Florida. As an example, Chicago experiences more than 50 murders every weekend, while New York City over 15. Las Vegas and the City of Phoenix experience less than 18 deaths from handguns per year, as per 2016 data.

Any one sustaining that the presence of the firearms increases the frequency and the intensity of all types of criminal activities, needs to examine the statistics compiled by the law enforcement agencies.

The distinction between "loaded guns" and just guns varies from jurisdiction to jurisdiction. Some legal authorities affirm that a "loaded gun" means exclusively a firearm with a round in the chamber. Others sustain that a gun does not need to have a round in the chamber to be considered fully loaded.

From a safety point of view, and for practical reasons, every gun needs to be considered fully loaded, when you do first see it, or touch it.

The constitutional implications of the gun-carrying situations are not as complex as some attorneys lead you to believe. Open carry practices raise most issues as to their constitutional aspects, however, they have never been totally ruled out as a definite right under the Second Amendment of the US Constitution, by any court decision. In a famous case, the District of Columbia v Heller, in 1980, speaking for the Supreme Court of the US, Justice Antonin Scalia said that:

"We find that the elements of the Second Amendment clearly guarantee the individual right to possess and carry weapons, in case of confrontations. However, like any other rights, the Second Amendment stipulations are not unlimited. No one has the right to keep and carry weapons whatsoever, and in any desirable manner whatsoever."

Forty five states recognize and secure their residents' right to keep and bear arms, in some fashion or another, and none of them prohibits the open carry practice.

Five states specifically charge their legislatures to come up with some sort of regulations – in 2015 - for open carry, and for concealed carry, to reflect closer all the federal law mandates regarding firearms.

Generally, there are no restrictions on the purchase of any type of firearms, (with few exemptions), and most states will record all such transactions by their type, brand, caliber, and serial number, in the files of the state's data bases set up within certain Public Safety Departments or in the Justice Department's Automated Firearm Recording Systems.

There is no consistency or synchronization in this process of complying with the federal law, fact which causes some notorious criminals to operate "under the radar".

The most shocking event, along this line, is offered by the North Hollywood bank robbery perpetrated by two bandits, armed with sophisticated weapons, wearing body armor, on February 28, 1997, when Larry Phillips, Jr. and Emil Matasareanu attempted to rob the Bank of America. On that occasion it was proved that a police force outgunned by the bad guys cannot be effective in facing such type of crime

In the ensuing gun battle over 1,800 rounds of armor-piercing bullets were fired by the bank robbers upon the Los Angeles SWAT team. In order to overcome the bandits, the police chief requisitioned several weapons from a sporting goods store, near the bank. Using AR-15, AK-47, and other types of firearms, the Los Angeles police force was finally able to subdue the bandits, after one hour-long engagement. The two bank robbers died, and 18 police officers were quite seriously injured. The policemen were armed with their standard semi-automatic 9.0 mm pistols or the .38 special revolvers, while the two bandits, used several fully automatic firearms, a Norinco Type 56 S, similar to an AK-47 assault rifle, a Bushmaster XM-15 Dissipator, and a HK-91, with a drum capable to hold 120 rounds that could penetrate police vehicles, and Kevlar body armor.

This incident sparked fierce debates between liberal and conservative factions in the media and in the state legislative bodies.

The conservative position was that the local police force needs to have its firearms dotation upgraded so that it can stand an assault from the criminal elements. A Colt .38 caliber revolver is no match for any AK-47, capable to fire 30 rounds per second!

The liberal media and left-leaning politicians objected to the this proposal to have police patrolmen better armed, on account of resembling an action of militarization of their civilian police forces, without an effective increase in the safety factors for the local civilians.

After almost 20 years, the same debate still remains unsettled, while the elements of public safety are analyzed over and over, resulting in the proverbial" analysis paralysis"

That type of inaction always places all law professional enforcement agents in a position of inferiority vis-à-vis the armed criminals.

ANATOMY OF A BANK ROBBERY

Shortly after the opening of the doors, at around 9:10 a.m., on the day of February 28, i997, Larry Phillips, Jr. and Emil Masatareanu, did enter to rob the Bank of America branch in North Hollywood, where they were confronted by three squad cars of the Los Angeles Police.

The ensuing shootout, between the bank robbers and the police, moved to an adjacent side street, while the two bandits attempted to flee the scene, Phillips on foot, and Matasareanu in the getaway vehicle. All this time, they did exchange heavy fire. In spite of his Kevlar body armor, Phillips was mortally wounded and committed suicide, right in front of the bank that he just robbed.

Phillips and Matasareanu were suspected to have also robbed several other Banks, in California, Arizona, and in Colorado, using the very same "modus operandi".

Due to the large number of injuries, weapons used, rounds fired, and money taken by the robbers, this tragic incident was regarded as the bloodiest event in the annals of police history. The bandits shot more than 1,200 rounds from their high-power rifles and pistols, at the LA police, and the officers responded with over 700 rounds from handguns.

Larry Eugene Phillips, Jr., (1970-1997), and his accomplice, Emil Decebal Matasareanu, (1966-1997), had dissimilar backgrounds and met in the Gold's Gym, in Venice, California, where they discovered their common hobbies: weight lifting, firearms, bank, and armored car hoists.

Larry Eugene Phillips, Jr. was a high school dropout, with serious knowledge in the area of computer technology, while Emil Decebal Matasareanu, born in Romania, was an electrical engineer trained in the USA. He attempted to run a computer repair service in Los Angeles, which never could produce any of the profits envisioned, and the two of them decided to obtain money on a much shorter path.

Consequently, in July 1993 they robbed an armored car making cash deliveries, right in front of the First Bank of Littleton, Colorado. That netted them over $ 200,000 in bills of various denominations.

The two of them were arrested, in October 1993, for speeding, in the Los Angeles area of Glendale, on the north-east side of that city.

After searching the vehicle, the police officers found several hand-guns and an assortment of high-power semi-automatic rifles, over 1,000 rounds of ammunition, police radio scanners, smoke bombs, and plastic explosives. The cops also discovered also in the trunk of their car several California license plates. They were charged with the intent to commit robbery, and the public defender assigned to them was able to convince Judge David Cohen, of the California Superior Court of Los Angeles, to consider the only 100 days served in jail, proportional to the offense, and placed them on a three year probation. After their release from jail they had all their confiscated property returned, with the exception of the firearms.

In June 1995, the pair ambushed a Brinks armored car killing one guard, Herman Cook, and injured the driver, who survived the attack. On that occasion they stole more than 1.5 million dollars. In May 1996 they robbed two branches of the Bank of America in the San Fernando Valley area of the Los Angeles, filling up the trunk of their 1987 white Chevrolet Celebrity with another $ 500,000. Phillips and Matasareanu soon got into the center of the NCIC FBI files, being dubbed as "high-incident bandits", by the investigators who did work on their case.

Contrary to the opinions vented in the media, the two bandits were not just some simple amateurs. They gathered a lot of precise, detailed data, about their targets, reconnoitered all the surrounding areas, to discover weak points in the security systems. Even if they had more than one million dollars in their possession, in November 1996, they made extensive preparations for the "next hit". They targeted several Bank of America branches, in Los Angeles, and around that city, and settled on the North Hollywood branch, which had only one 70-years-old man as a guard on duty. At about 9:05, the two of them entered the bank and swallowed some two or three pills of phenobarbital, a medication an MD prescribed to Matasareanu, as an anticonvulsive. They took those pills to calm their nerves. They set their watch alarms to 8 minutes.

That was the minimum response time they meticulously observed on the Los Angeles cops and studied on their police scanner.

As they entered the bank, the two of them were spotted by two Los Angeles police patrolmen, Loren Farrell and Martin Perello, from their patrol vehicle:

"15-A-43. Requesting back up, and assistance! We have a possible 211 in progress!" 211 was the police code for an armed robbery.

As the bandits entered the bank, they forced a customer using the ATM, and all others to the floor and shot several rounds into the ceiling in an attempt to terrorize the bank employees, and the costumers, which were standing in line to the teller windows:

"This is a f...ing bank robbery! Everybody hit the floor! Now!"

They shot to pieces the "bullet proof" glass door and entered behind the tellers' counter and to the vault. That security partition, made out of inch-thick glass was meant to stop handgun bullets, but not the armor-piercing AK-47, HK-91, or the Bushmaster rounds. The robbers forced the bank assistant manager, John Villigrana, to open the vault and to fill the canvas bags they had, with bills. Due to the fact that the day before, the bank cashed a lot of payroll checks to people in the neighborhood, the bank cash reserve in the vault was quite low. When Phillips and Matasareanu saw that there was much less than the one million dollars they did expect, one of them discharged the entire drum of 75 rounds from his HK-91, into the vault, destroying most of its contents. They left with something like 300,000 dollars.

Outside the bank, the first responders took strategic defensive positions at the four corners of the bank building, taking cover behind their squad cars.

At 9:30 Phillips exited the front door of the bank, as possibly to survey the police position, while being ordered, through megaphones, to drop his weapons and to surrender. He turned around and reentered the bank. Just a couple of minutes later, Phillips exited the south door of the bank building and Matasareanu fled through the north door. All this time the two bank robbers fired furiously their automatic weapons on the cops. The police officers were armed with Beretta 9 mm, Glock 9 mm, and Smith and Wesson .38 caliber handguns, which were totally useless against the Aramid/Kevlar body armor strengthened with plates of high grade steel. The only vulnerable part of the robbers' bodies, were their heads, but due to those particular circumstances, the police couldn't do hardly anything else.

The heavy barrage of automatic fire coming from the robbers, kept the cops pinned down behind their vehicles, while the guns they used did not offer the range or the accuracy necessary to attempt head shots on the two bank robbers. A couple dozen officers and civilians were hurt during the following ten or twelve minutes, after which Matasareanu got into his car, urging Phillips to follow him. Phillips hesitated until his hand and his HK-

91magazine got hit by a police bullet. Unable to use his powerful AK-47 rifle anymore, he retrieved from the trunk of his white Chevrolet Celebrity trunk, the Norinco type 56 S-1, and continued to fire wildly.

After several calls for "officer down", the Los Angeles Police SWAT team was deployed in full force, to the parking lot of the North Hollywood Bank of America.

At around 9:50 AM the police shot again Phillips in the right hand making it impossible for him to shoot back at the police. With his left hand he fired one round under his chin and fell down. The police continued to shoot at him for several more minutes.

One of the members of the SWAT team, hiding under a police car, took aim and shot at Matasareanu's legs, a part of his body not protected by body armor. He raises his hands up in surrender.

All this time, several television crews broadcast live the entire ordeal of that confrontation between two armed bank robbers and the Los Angeles Police Department. Phillips died due to a self-inflicted gun wound to the head, while he bled profusely from seven or eight shots to his legs and arms. Matasareanu, cursing heavily the cops, kept trying to incite the copse to take his life out. There were too many policemen and civilians who needed emergency medical attention, and by the time the bank robbers were placed into an ambulance, it was too late. They were both dead. Scenes filmed from the air by news helicopters revealed in detail the devastation and the damages inflicted upon a quiet community by two misfits.

Most all of the weapons in the arsenal of Larry Phillips, Jr. and Emil Matasareanu, used in the robbery of the Bank of America in North Hollywood on the February 28, 1997, did not come from legitimate firearm dealers. No matter what kind of background checks one may have undertaken, it would have been impossible to prevent those two bandits from obtaining that tremendous fire power they used against the Los Angeles Police.

As a result of this incident, the debate about gun control gained more intensity, with the liberal media, and the leftist politicians pointing out to the failure of the state background checks in the American democracy.

The gun control opponents concluded that it was the failure of the government to enforce the law, that precipitated this tragedy, yet both factions were wrong. No one could have anticipated and prevented what happened that fateful day in North Hollywood, even though all the data pointed directly to the state's judicial system.

The two bandits never got the proper justice, in a setting in which the police was always handicapped by a "revolving-door" justice system approach, in which the criminals are given a slap on the wrist, and are returned into the society to continue their crimes.

No political state subdivision ever questions the judges' actions, even if all characteristics of judicial work point out to the marked tendency of some justices to legislate from the bench, in contradiction to constitutional principles.

The judges, both at state and federal levels, are totally immune to prosecution for their gross negligence in failing to remove from the society the persons incapable of ever being rehabilitated. It seems that our judges are more concerned with the comfort of the criminals, than with the welfare of the victims.

The brazen and daring attack on a bank, in the middle of a city congested with people and vehicles, caused causes for the heads of neighboring police departments to reconsider al their procedures of responding to such crimes. The SWAT team response was thoroughly analyzed, and it was found quite inadequate.

The legitimate question of type of firearms were needed to avoid placing the police in an inferiority position, became an urgent issue for the state legislators in Sacramento. As a result, the police departments in many states got to be equipped with AR-15.

The specialists in the media, who followed the entire North Hollywood bank robbery on TV, beamed down from news stations helicopters, revealed the shocking truth that many police and sheriff departments were not equipped to withstand such an attack.

They placed the blame on the judicial system that operated at a flagrant disconnect from reality, by giving the criminals just a slap on the wrist, sending them back in the society to continue their crime careers.

ANATOMY OF A MASSACRE

The Sandy Hook Elementary School, or the SHES, massacre occurred on December 14, 2012, in Newtown, Connecticut, where the 20-years-old, Adam Lanza, of the same town, mortally shot 20 children and 6 adult staff members. Just before getting to that elementary school, he shot and killed his mother, in her own home.

This tragic event was qualified as the deadliest mass shooting in a school by a single gunman.

A November 2013 report, issued by the Connecticut's Attorney General concluded unequivocally that Adam Lanza acted alone, and did plan all his actions in advance, paying attention to absolutely all details of that abject act. The investigators could not establish why Lanza did what he did, or why he selected the Sandy Hook Elementary School. He took to his grave all the elements of the motivation for his crime, after he committed suicide. No one will ever know why he selected to massacre so many innocents, most of them children.

The time table of the Newtown events of December 14, 2012 can be quite significant in examining what happened, and when. On the day of December 13, 2012, around 1:30 PM it was reported that Adam Lanza entered into a heated argument with the head teacher there, who forced him to leave the school premises immediately. It seems that the subsequent investigation failed to mention what actually did happen, at that elementary school, when the 20-years-old was evicted off campus. Next day he returned with definite plans for revenge, just as soon as he killed his mother, and took her firearms with him. All the remaining elements are just pure speculation, and none of the people who studied the timetable of that event could definitely point out to a motive or any cause indicative of the rage that young man could have been capable of:

9:30 a.m., the shooter enters the Elementary School;

9:36 a.m., the Newtown Police receives the first call;

9:37 a.m., the police dispatcher broadcasts the 911 call just received from the school;

9:39 a.m., local police and state police dispatched to the school;

9:40 a.m., two more squad cars arrive at the school;

9:42 a.m., last firearm shot heard at the school;

9:45 a.m., the school is placed in lockdown;

9:50 a.m., the evacuation of pupils and teachers begins, under State Police supervision.

In approximately 20 minutes, the entire ordeal was over. The local police and the State Police, used helicopters, tracking dogs, to comb the facility from the air and from the ground, for eventual any other accomplices, bombs, booby-traps, etc.

The New York City medical examiner dispatched, the next day, a mobile morgue, to Newtown, with a complement of specialists, who during the following week would compile a surprising autopsy report, which baffled all the authorities:

"There were no traces of alcohol or any drugs found in Adam Lanza's tissues, while his brain and nervous system was free from ills, tumors, cancer, or abnormal physiological aspects. All the toxicological test returned were negative."

The case was investigated by a multitude of states and federal agencies which focused on both, the site and off site studies. There was no suicide note, nor any indication of premeditation even if all the specialists suspected that such circumstances existed.

Just prior to leaving his house, Lanza destroyed his computer hard drive, to obscure any possible indications about the places he visited on the Internet. The forensic specialists could only retrieve a small part of the data Lanza searched on the web. Most of the places he visited were all related to other mass shootings, like those in Norway in 2011, the 2006 Amish School shootings in Nickel Mines, Pennsylvania, and the 1999 Colorado Columbine School massacre.

The investigators were perplexed to find so many bits and pieces of apparently connected elements, resulted from Lanza's research into several mass shootings, and for the ways to commit suicide by gun. Definitely, there emerged the blurred portrait of a troubled young man, who rejected any authority, including that of his own mother, and prepared his own exit from this society, "with a bang". Such a contorted outline of human psychiatry can be difficult to ascertain and the frequency at which it occurs, is not indicative of common crimes.

The complete circumstances of this massacre need to be examined through the magnifying glasses of the local school security arrangements. The Sandy Hook Elementary School was a "gun-free zone", and the entry to the front of the school was kept "secure" at all time, under lock and key, while the perpetrator, Adam Lanza, seems to have known all entry codes.

That morning around 9:30 AM, Lanza killed his mother in her own bedroom, with a .22 caliber bolt action Savage MK II-F rifle, and drove to the Sandy Hook Elementary School, in Newtown, Connecticut. There he found the front door locked, and with a volley of bullets from a fully loaded automatic rifle, a Bushmaster XM-15 E2S, he gained entry into the school building. That rifle belonged to his mother. Clad in black clothes, he was wearing steel rimmed dark sunglasses, yellow earplugs, and in the pockets of his green windbreaker he carried some 10 to 12 magazines for that Bushmaster rifle. Original reports that he was wearing some type of body armor proved later to be false. The first shots reverberated throughout the school halls, and through the public address systems, yet nobody realized that the sounds heard were gunshots fired just outside the principal's office.

The school principal, Natalie Hammond, Dawn Hochsprung, the school psychologist, Mary Sherlach, and three other teachers who were all participating in a work meeting in the main office, stopped the meeting and sent two janitors out to investigate the origin of that noise, which resembled firecrackers.

The school janitor, Rick Thorne, yelled as loud as he could: "Put the gun down!" and was shot several times, but survived. Next, Lanza killed Dawn Hochsprung and Mary Sherlach, but he failed to kill Natalie Hammond, who with several wounds to her legs crawled to the room in which they had that work session, and held the metallic door locked, to prevent Lanza's entry there. She survived.

Failing to find anyone in the school offices, because the people were hiding behind their desks, the shooter started to sweep the area, with his rifle's sights, getting into the other adjacent hallways. Diane Day, the school therapist recalled later that she heard a lot of screams followed by rapid fire. A substitute kindergarten teacher, who went to secure the door of her classroom, was hit by a bullet in the foot while several rifle-fired bullets ricocheted all around her. Lanza never entered her classroom. After moving to the next classroom, where a young substitute teacher, Lauren Rousseau worked, he found that she herded away all her first graders, and was trying to hide them, assisted by Rachel D'Avino, a new hire. Lanza shot both dead, together with some 5 children. There was only one single survivor from that group of first graders, a six-years-old girl. Entering another first grade classroom, that of Victoria Leigh Soto. Lanza walked to the back of that room, where he discovered that Soto hid some nine pupils under the desks. He shot all of them dead.

Victoria Leigh Soto placed herself between the shooter and the children, yelling at them, to run out of that classroom. Lanza killed her. Anne Marie Murphy, Soto's teacher aide, who worked with special-needs children, covered with her body a six-year-old boy, who was also shot to death. Nine of the students Soto was teaching ran outside the class-room and survived.

The school nurse, Sally Cox, 60, hid under her desk narrowly escaping to be shot, while she watched Lanza's boots moving two feet away from where she was.

The school secretary, Barbara Halstead called "911" and hid in a utility closet in her office, frozen in terror for hours. The custodian, Rick Thorne, ran all over the school to warn the rest of the teachers about the presence of a shooter on premises. Due to his efforts, over 32 children survived, in the library, and many others in the adjacent classrooms. The librarians, Yvonne Czech and Maryann Jacob, pushed 18 children into a storage room in the back of the library, where the shooter failed to notice them. The first grade teacher, Kaitlin Roig hid 14 children in a bathroom and barricaded the door.

In total, Lanza killed eight boys, twelve girls, all between the ages of six and seven, and six adult teachers. All the shootings occurred in the first-grade classes, where some victims were shot multiple times. One boy, Noah Pozner, just 6-years-old, had 15 bullet wounds in his torso and head.

The authorities determined that during his shooting rampage, Lanza reloaded his Bushmaster frequently, firing only 15-round bursts out of his 30-round magazines. Few of the bullets, fired in the first-grade classrooms, nearest to the school entrance, reached the school parking lot damaging some of the staff's vehicles.

The last shot rang out around 9:40 AM, from Lanza's Glock 20 SF, a 9 mm semiautomatic Austrian-made pistol. The shooter committed suicide in the classroom nr. 10.

The final report on this hideous event was issued by the state and federal authorities, on November 25, 2013, reaching the conclusion that Adam Lanza acted alone, and that he did not exhibit any specific ideological affinity, other than his own "pathogenic obsession with mass murders". There were some indications that this shooter planned well in advance all his actions, being familiar with various types of weapons and ammunition. He did not have a criminal record. As a result of Sandy Hook Elementary School shooting, several national organizations called for a reassessment of the gun laws in the USA, proposing the ban of many new categories of weapons, and the universal background checks on the purchases of all firearms. Adam Lanza however, never did purchase any kind of weapon. His parents did.

A report issued by the Office of that State's Children's Advocate, in November 2014, said that Lanza had Asperger's syndrome and as a teenager suffered from deep depression, anxiety, and a severe case of obsessive-compulsive disorder, but concluded that they may had not "caused nor led to his murderous acts." The report went on to say: "His severe and deteriorating internalized mental health issues, combined with an atypical preoccupation with violence and access to deadly weapons provided the recipe for mass murder".

The Asperger syndrome is a severe developmental disorder characterized by significant difficulties in social interaction and in non-verbal communications, along with some restrictive patterns of behavior and interests.

If you analyze all the mass shootings described in the literature published for the law enforcement people you, would find that the greatest majority of shooters, over 99%, were afflicted by mental problems of various severity.

The dominant characteristic of the people who commit mass murders, is the anti-social attitude, coupled with a deep feeling of inadequacy in personal relationships, and severe depression, conditions extremely difficult to diagnose and to treat, as mental illnesses.

How can anybody prepare for the unpredictable?

In the case of the Sandy Hook Elementary School, any person could see the large signs posted at both end of the street proclaiming in large red font that;

"This is a gun and drug free school zone!"

That was like advertising to the shooter that he could do his dirty deed calmly, since no one would shoot back at him. And that is the main argument for allowing some trustworthy school employees or security guards to be properly trained to respond to such emergencies with an active shooter on the premises. The cost of extra security measures should not be an issue vis-à-vis the children's safety.

Surveillance video cameras work well however, there is rarely anyone to monitor them. Usually that causes response delays, and the information can be examined much later, after everything is already done.

There is no "bullet-proof" method to deal with shooting emergencies in schools, and new gun control laws, of the type envisioned by the leftists are not the answer. If one of the school's janitors would have had a gun, when he first came across Lanza, many of those children's lives would have been saved... When a tragedy like that at the Sandy Hook School happens, it is not sufficient to only analyze it, and to compile the crime statistics. We need to be able to educate effectively the educators in how to act if something like that happens. The life of a child is priceless!

RESISTING CRIMINAL ATTACKS

The relatively popular opinion that only the men are "good with guns", is a sexist fallacy, which ignores the thousands of ladies, who are an important part of our military, law enforcement, and of the shooting sports.

A 25-years old beauty queen, in Florida, Meghan Brown, was suddenly awaken, in the middle of the night, in her Tierra Verde home, by someone breaking her back door and forcing his way in.

Confronting the intruder, she was knocked to the ground, dragged by her hair, and suffered face injuries from the criminal's kicks. Her fiancé, awaken also by the noise, jumped to defend her. That caused the intruder to turn away from Meghan, and she took the opportunity to retrieve a handgun from a drawer, after which she fired two shots, killing the home invader.

The bandit, the 42-years-old Albert Franklin Hill, it turned out, after the police arrived, to be a habitual criminal with a lengthy criminal record, which included rapes, robberies, grand theft and manslaughter. He was just released from prison one week earlier, after he served eight years out of a sentence of twelve years. The County Attorney found that homicide justified, as a bona-fide self-defense, and no charges were filed against Meghan Brown, or her fiancé.

That was one of the many cases that occur daily, in which a law-abiding citizen has to use a gun to survive a criminal's attack, and no reasonable mind would argue against this use of firearms.

Another example of criminals using guns, while law-abiding citizen were sitting ducks, is offered by the Luby's massacre. The Luby's mass shooting took place on October 16, 1991, at a Luby's Cafeteris, in Killeen, Texas,

The perpetrator, George Hennard, 35, drove his blue Ford Ranger pickup truck through the front window of the restaurant, after which he rapidly shot and killed 23 people, and wounded 27 others. He had a brief shootout with the police, and refused to obey their orders to surrender, fatally shooting himself.

Ranked at the time as the deadliest mass shooting in Texas, its death toll was only surpassed by that of the Virginia Tech mass shooting of April 2007. As of February 2018, this incident ranked as the sixth-deadliest shooting in the US by a single shooter.

It was National Boss's Day, and the cafeteria was crowded to full capacity. At first, bystanders thought the crash of that truck was just an accident, but after Hennard started shooting, some patrons tried to escape from the cafeteria, almost immediately. The first victim was a local veterinarian, Dr. Michael Griffith while another patron, one Tommy Vaughn, threw himself through a rear window, sustaining multiple injuries, but thus creating an escape avenue for himself, and for some 50 other cafeteria patrons.

Hennard was described by the few people who knew him, as reclusive and belligerent, with an explosive temper. He had been kicked out of the Merchant Marine because of his possession and use of marijuana and other drugs on the job. Numerous reports included a few accounts of Hennard's expressed extreme hatred for women, which included his own mother. An ex-roommate of his said that:

"He hated Blacks, Hispanics, gays, and married people. He believed that all women were snakes, and always had few derogatory remarks about them, especially after fights with his mother".

Some survivors of that cafeteria shootings said that Hennard had passed over men, to shoot only women. 14 of the 23 people killed were women, as were many of the wounded. He called some of them "vipers", "bitches" and "whores", before he did shoot them to death.

The Glock C-17, 9 mm, and the Rugger P-8, 9 mm pistols, which Hennard used to kill Luby's patrons, were both legally purchased, during February or March 1991 at a gun shop in Henderson, NV.

One of the Luby's customers, on that tragic day, was a Texas chiropractor, Dr. Suzanna Gratia Hupp, who was having a meal with her parents, when a small blue pickup truck burst through the cafeteria's front glass plates. The irony of those circumstances consists in the fact that Dr. Hupp always did carry a handgun in her purse, but this time, apprehensive of falling on the wrong side of the law, she locked it in the trunk of her car, a decision that she regretted for the rest of her life. In response to the trauma of losing both her parents due to a criminal act, she became a vocal activist for allowing concealed weapons in Texas.

Incidentally, exactly at the same time, an anti-crime bill was scheduled for a vote in the US House of Representatives the day after the Luby's massacre.

Some of the Hennard victims had been constituents of Representative Chet Edwards, and in response he abandoned his opposition to a gun control provision that was part of that bill. The provision, which did not pass, would have banned some weapons and magazines like the ones used by Hennard.

The NRA, Texas State Rifle Association, and others preferred that the state allows its citizens to carry concealed handguns, with full support from Dr. Hupp, now an elected member to the Texas House of Representatives.

The Democratic Texas governor, Ann Richards, vetoed that bills, but in 1995, her Republican successor, George W. Bush, signed the concealed carry law in Texas. Dr. Suzanna Hupp, who was present at the Luby's, where both her parents were killed, worked hard to get elected in the Texas House of Representatives, so that she could initiate the passing of the concealed gun carry law. She later testified that she would have liked to have had her gun, but said, "It was a hundred feet away, in my car" (she had feared that if she was caught carrying it, she might lose her chiropractor's license). She testified across the country in support of concealed handgun laws, and was elected to the Texas House of Representatives for five consecutive terms in 1996.

She wrote a best-seller, "From Luby's to the State Legislature: One Woman's Fight against Gun Control" which was published by the Privateer Publications of San Antonio, Texas. Dr. Hupp has been quoted in such publications, as US News & World Report, The Wall Street Journal, Texas Monthly, Time, New York Times, People Magazine, and many others, in addition to being featured on several TV news programs, like the 48 Hours, World News Tonight, and 60 Minutes. What a lady!

We all have mothers, wives, and daughters, and we all consider family safety a matter of national security! Is there anyone, who thinks that women still can't measure up to men's "standards", when it comes to determination in face of the dangers thrust upon them by the criminal element?

In our society the women are absolutely equal to men, in every single respect, and treating them as the second-class citizens of our country, is an ill throw-back from the dark ages.

There are some immigrant groups in the US who profess, in striking fashion, that the women are inferior to men and use force to prove that.

The so called "honor killings", which result in the murder of wives or daughters for obscure reasons, form an integral part, as an example of the Muslim society's traditions. Many times a young lady was murdered with the consent of both her parents, for trying to date a young man, who was not a Muslim. In other cases, the wife was punished by death, for insisting to go to college.

The value of the life of a woman, is a notion that many such primitive groups cannot comprehend.

FATAL GUN ATTRACTION

It is a well-known fact that firearms exercise a lethal attraction to children, especially to boys. That's why any gun owner has to be extremely cautious to insure that no children have access to firearms.

During the 2016 school year, over 500 children under the age of 12, were expelled from schools, for bringing guns to school, in their backpacks. Luckily, only three, of those cases resulted in deaths, while six children were injured.

How did, those children, get hold of handguns?

Most likely, from their parents!

Some psychologists recommend that the parents instill in their children an attitude of serious fear and respect for all kinds of firearms, through a process of education that needs to start early. Of course, responsible parents do everything possible to remove the chances of children getting hold of guns. That implies the use of secure places, verifiably not accessible to children, such as gun safes, under lock and key, and trigger locks.

However, no matter how "child-proof" one may think that the place where the firearms are may be, often a child, most likely under the age of 12, would find a way to defeat any safety measures. And when that happens, the seeds of adult negligence may germinate into horrible tragedies.

The best approach to this issue is to condition the kids to realize that the guns are not toys, and messing with them is punished in ways that cut off the appetite to play with them.

When the children grow to an age of reasoning, usually at 12-years of age, it is advisable to take them to the shooting range to teach them the safety of firearm handling. Some of the youth clubs, sponsored by the NRA, or the Boy Scouts of America, are excellent places to insure that the children do not break the safety rules generally set by the parents.

However, many single-parent families lack the father figure, and the children get most of their education on the street, under the lethal influence of youth gangs. That's the place where they get exposed to the idea that only a gun can make them "important", and they do not hesitate to use it, as a "sign of maturity". The only attempts to correct this social disease presented by children with guns, comes from the overburdened juvenile justice system, yet the guns remain in the hands of children and adolescents. And one wonders how come lately we witness a lot of school shootings that take an unacceptable toll in lost young lives. The explanation is the proliferation and the abundance of firearms available to people who should not touch them. Add to this the mental issues that many youngsters suffer from, and you will see that our modern society will never be able to stamp out the gun violence caused by children or directed toward them. The notion of "children" most likely includes any persons under 18, with very few exceptions, when the children commit "adult crimes".

SURVIVING A HOME INVASION

When Yolanda Rousseau, of Kenner, Louisiana, turned onto the old street where her little house was, she noticed a group of four or five men, but she did not pay too much attention to their presence. That was primarily a black part of the city, and one or two young Black men in the neighborhood did not warrant additional scrutiny. She knew from her own experience, that many young Black men are thieves of opportunity, naturally inclined to commit various mischievous acts, yet the 65-years-old grandmother was not too worried. Ever since she obtained her permit to carry a handgun, she kept her head high, determined to resist any kind of attempts to intimidate her, or to limit her freedom in the city that she loved. During the last ten years, or so, she had no reason to think that she would ever become a crime victim.

She parked her white 2014 Ford Focus in the driveway, on her usual spot, next to the one her daughter would park, checked the mail box, and entered her house with a handful of envelopes and magazines. Seated at the kitchen table, she scanned the mail just received, and got her shoes off, sighing with relief, when her feet enjoyed a little bit of freedom from confinement. Her only daughter, Nadine, was out of town for the next couple of days, and since they lived alone in that house, she turned on the TV, for company. It was shortly after 6:00 PM and the mews bulletin was talking about the sharp increase in the violent crime in the New Orleans area.

She knew that a significant part of state of Louisiana was predominantly Democratic, and favored leftist causes, yet she was convinced that most Black, like herself, were conservative. She reasoned that:

"If you work for your money, have a house for which you pay mortgage, go to church regularly, like sports, and own a hunting rifle, or a pistol, you are conservative woman, no matter what others do or say."

Often, she'd talk with her daughter, Nadine, about the changes in peoples' attitudes that followed the Katrina hurricane, of August 2005, when the quality of life there took a dive.

It seems that only a handful of original Kenner people did remain in her neighborhood, most being replaced by those who came from all over the creation, from New York, and other large cities, like Miami, Chicago, Memphis, or Atlanta. Louisiana definitely lost her traditionally unhurried, peaceful life that anyone associated with the "speak easy" culture of the past. She missed that dearly.

Working in a local bank, she heard numerous stories about elderly people being robbed in plain daylight, or had their cars hijacked. That's why she applied for a concealed handgun permit, after spending a couple of weekends in a special training class. There she learned how to shoot, and how to differentiate between the situations which justify deadly force, and those which do not. While waiting for her license to carry a concealed gun, she was terrified by what happened to one lady, living probably less than four blocks away from her house. That case was broadcast as a news item one evening, and concerned a retired bank employee who applied for a license, in view of the fact that local gangs often victimized the elderly. She was murdered in front of her own house, while waiting for the license that would have allowed her to defend herself with a gun in such a situation.

Yolanda Rousseau did not want anything like that to happen to her. She religiously carried, her Beretta 9 mm pistol in her purse, in a little pouch which on its outside had transparent pockets which displayed her makeup kit.

She gained a different demeanor after she obtained her concealed gun license. She kept her head up, never showed any kind of fear or hesitation, when some unsavory character crossed her path and acted provocatively. She was quite sure of herself, and the criminal element knew not to mess with little old ladies who did not show fear toward anyone, who was thinking to snatch a purse.

It was shortly after 7:30 PM when her doorbell rang. She opened the door, and there were Bob and Pamela, two of her best friends, who, returning home from shopping and dropped in, just to chat a little. Pleasantly surprised by that visit, she noticed a group of four teenagers on the other side of the street, but she did not pay additional attention to that scene, even if those youngsters seemed not to belong there. As she served her guests some peach cobbler and iced water, talking and laughing, the front door burst open and three youngsters got in wielding knives. The fourth individual did remain outside, probably as a look-out.

Bob jumped up in the defense of the two ladies and was stabbed in the chest. Yolanda bent down, picked her purse, and asked ironically:

"Do you want my money?"

"Give me your purse, you bitch!"

Yolanda reached in her purse and withdrew her 9 mm handgun firing two deadly shots. Two of the surviving tugs took off at an impressive speed. After calling the 911, the ambulance medical emergency personnel stopped Bob's hemorrhage and transported him to the emergency room. The police compiled a lengthy report, took several photograph of the scene, and of the cadavers of the two dead criminals, drawing sketches of Yolanda's house. They called the night judge who ruled the two homicides as justified. In the state of Louisiana deadly force is permitted in order to prevent any situations that may result in injury or death.

After verifying the identity of the two dead bandits, the local police found out that the two dead men were quite known to police, as having an extremely long criminal record, which included robbery, rape, grand theft, and car-jacking. They have been just released from the Angola prison, after serving five years for violent crimes. Their two accomplices were soon found, and arrested by the Kenner police.

A local TV station wanted to ask Yolanda Rousseau for an interview for their evening crime monitoring program, but she refused to do it. It was a very sad situation, she thought, that she needed to waste two young lives, but, on the other hand, her life was just as precious, and defending it, was a God-given right.

After a couple of days spent in the hospital, following some surgery to fix a severed artery, Bob was allowed to go home, where he filed a state application for a concealed gun permit. His wife, Pamela did the same thing. Three weeks later they were in a classroom, studying the correct ways to behave with a gun.

The neighborhood homeowners association purchased and placed at both ends of her street some signs proclaiming in red letters: "This is not a gun free zone. Criminal may get to be prosecuted to the full extent of the law, if they survive the confrontations with the local residents."

It seems that those sign worked well. No hoodlums hanged around anymore in that neighborhood. They moved their "hunting grounds", from residential areas, to the malls, and to the central shopping centers.

An armed citizen is one of the best deterrents for crime. It is a verifiable fact that in states that allow open carry of handguns, the incidence of gun violence is much lower than in the states that limit that. Criminals would rarely risk to select a victim that could shoot back!

And that is a fact of our modern life…

ANATOMY OF A CARJACKING

Marla Thomas, 59, a resident of Pasadena, Texas, had a daily commute of some 20 miles to her place of work, at a law firm. On the day of March 8, 2017 while exiting the freeway 59, she stopped at a traffic light, some three feet behind the car in front of her. She had all the doors locked, and she was surprised to see a young man, breaking the passenger side window with the gun he had in his hand, reached in, opened the passenger door and jumped in:

"Drive bitch!"

She knew she was in trouble when the light turned green and she followed the traffic. She couldn't do anything but follow the commands of that hoodlum. When the carjacker ordered her to make a right turn into a side street, she spotted a highway patrolman giving a ticket to some driver. She took that opportunity to ram the policeman's car. With the gun drawn the trooper got both of them on the ground, and while handcuffing the carjacker, Marla told him what happened. The cop retrieved the gun from the floor of Marla's car, where the criminal dropped it, and called for backup.

On that occasion it was found that the perpetrator of that crime had a long police record which included battery, burglary, carjacking, and manslaughter, after completing eight years of a ten-year sentence. He was on parole at that time. Marla escaped with her life, and some $ 5,000 worth of damages, which the insurance only reimbursed her partially.

The first thing she did, the same very day, was to apply for a concealed gun permit with the Texas Department of Public Safety.

It took her less than one full month to go through the classroom training, shooting instruction on the out of town range, and finally when she had her gun in the purse, her confidence was once more revived.

During the training she received in the classroom, she took a lot of notes, just like for the briefings she worked for her lawyers, with copious details. Periodically she would review her notes, and thus coming with some worthwhile conclusions, regarding some of the possible carjacking scenarios:

While driving through a high-crime area, be aware of your surroundings. Always keep at least a distance of one car length from the vehicle in front of you, at traffic lights, or stop signs. This way you will have enough space to be able to speed away in an emergency of the type she just experienced in Pasadena.

Pay close attention to your surrounding areas, entering into parking garages, drive-through places, ATMs, or shopping centers, because that's where most carjacking cases occur. If you see any people just lurking around, drive away. When using an ATM, do not linger there to count the money, or to put them in your wallet or purse, just drive away.

If you are walking toward your car, on a parking lot, or in a parking garage, and someone demands your car keys, toss them as far as you can, in an opposite direction from your vehicle, and run toward the entry or exit doors where you may see other people. Do keep a spare set of car keys in your purse, on you. That would be your insurance policy if someone takes your keys out of your hand.

If you are stopped at a traffic light or at a stop sign, and you see someone approaching your car, especially at night, drive away, even if that means driving on the sidewalk, or running a red light, provided that you can do that safely, without killing pedestrians.

If a carjacker gets into your car's passenger seat while you are stopped, immediately jump out of the car and run. If that same carjacker sticks a gun in your face, offer to surrender the car, and slam the breaks, get out of the car and run, ideally toward other people, or inside a building.

If a carjacker stick a gun or a knife through your open car window, while stopped, open the door and hit the criminal with it, while flooring the gas pedal, even if you hit the car in front of you. The carjacker would not expect that and may run away.

No matter what car you drive, always keep in mind that your own life is much more valuable than anything else. If your car gets bumped from behind, do not stop. Keep on driving to the first place that you can be assisted by customers or employees of any business nearby. Criminals usually use minor accidents to get the driver to stop to survey the damages, and rob the driver, often killing him or her, while getting away with the victim's vehicle.

If you carry a gun and are 100% sure that the other driver and his passengers would hurt you, shoot to kill, while disabling the criminal's car, with shots into the tires. If the criminals get away, do everything possible to retain the license plate number.

Every carjack situation is different, and the only thing you have to keep in mind, is your survival.

If you carry a gun, and the carjacker fires at you, move to be shielded by the engine of your vehicle, and fire back. Aim to kill, by sighting your gun toward the head or torso of the criminal(s).

Do not panic and act just like you did when you aimed at the targets on the shooting range, where you got your instruction to obtain a concealed gun license. Usually a carjacker will shoot to scare or to intimidate you. When faced by someone who would shoot back, a criminal would not be able to concentrate and will miss hitting you. You should not miss.

Your added advantage is that the noise of discharging guns will attract attention, and eventually would bring the police to save the day for you.

It is a sad reality of our times that the criminal element will always try to find victims that can be easily subdued and robbed at gun point. That includes women and senior citizens, who normally did not fight back, but that has changed.

After you obtained your concealed carry license, it is a very good idea to plan to go back on the shooting range, at least every other month to fire 25 to 50 rounds, to maintain and improve your shooting accuracy. Keep in mind that in a gun fight there are no winners, only survivors.

CRIME POLITICS

All sort of politicians, media "specialists", social engineers, good-intentioned people, and some not so good-intentioned, fan the issue of gun control, as a mean to curb gun violence. No matter what you think, you have to see that most of them do "bark at the wrong tree",

Instead of proposing new laws for gun control, while the laws already existing are not enforced, they should focus hard on crime control. Gun violence does not happen in a vacuum, but in an environment which allows crime to thrive, as an industry for illicit profits. Closing down crime enterprises can do much more than sterile philosophical debates on gun control.

Examine, for a moment, the most recent crime statistics compiled by various law enforcement agencies:

In 2017 Chicago had 2,987 gun-related injuries and 915 homicides, making it the murder capital of USA, followed by Detroit, with 1,975 gun-related injuries, and 573 homicides. By comparison, during the same period, New York City did record 1,421 gun related injuries and 495 homicides.

Los Angeles and the state of Maryland had also, high gun-related fatalities, but could not unseat Chicago for the first place.

It is quite interesting to see that the crime statistics are the highest in cities run by Democrat administrations, yet in, in New York City the crime rate decreased considerably from 1994 to

2014. In 1994 when Rudy Giuliani became mayor a massive effort was undertaken to reduce the crime rate and to improve the life of that city's dwellers.

In 1996, during his first term as mayor of the New York City, based on the legal precedent presented by the Terry v. Ohio case, of 1968, the city police was empowered to use "Terry Stops".

That name is derived from the case in which the Supreme Court of the USA held that police may briefly detain any person whom they reasonably suspect is involved in some criminal activity. The Supreme Court also held that police may do a limited search of the suspect's outer garments for weapons if they have a reasonable and articulable suspicion that the person detained may be "armed and dangerous."

To have reasonable suspicion that would justify a stop, police must be able to point to "specific and articulable facts" that would indicate to a reasonable police officer that the person stopped is or is about to be engaged in some criminal activity, as opposed to the proof of past conduct. Reasonable suspicion would depend on the "totality of circumstances", and it can result from a combination of facts, each of which may, by itself, be totally innocuous. The "Terry Stops", also called "Giuliani's Cleanup" removed during the first year over 2,900 hand guns out of the hands of felons, who were placed back in prison, since they were prohibited from owning any firearms.

Several other major cities did try to emulate the New York's example, with excellent results, except for Chicago. Consequently, the crime rate, in the Big Apple, dropped by 40%, for the first time since 1940. Rudi Giuliani was the mayor of New York City between 1994 and 2001, and was succeeded by Michael Blumberg, who tried to maintain the status quo, without rocking the boat. The next mayor, Bill de Blasio, elected in 2014, blamed, falsely, the increase in city violent crime there, on previous administrations. He set out to prove that the gun violence in the city of New York is due to illegal firearms coming in from out of state venues.

To prove his point, he selected three retired policemen to act as private detectives and sent them to Arizona and Texas, to try to demonstrate how easy it is to obtain illegal guns.

In Arizona they went the "Crossroads of the West" Gun Show in Phoenix, where no gun dealer would sell them any firearms, with their New York identification papers, that they could not tell if they were valid or not.

Next they went to the "Wild Weasel" Gun Show, in the town of Kingsland, Texas, where they attempted to purchase some ten firearms. The dealers there absolutely refused to sell anything to those "suspicious looking New York guys". Mayor's Bill de Blasio experiment turned out to be a $ 100,000 failure that the New York taxpayers could have gladly missed to foot the bill for.

The last mayor of the New York City seemed much more preoccupied with the comfort of the illegal immigrants and with the welfare of the criminals, by declaring that city a "sanctuary city", while the "Terry Stops" have been all discontinued, on account of possible civil right violations, even though the US Supreme Court set up exact parameters for implementation.

Under the constraints of several legal precedents, the police may randomly search vehicles, under the "plain view doctrine", and can seize and use as evidence, weapons or contraband visible from outside the vehicle. The New York City legal staff urged the local law enforcement personal to avoid doing that without a warrant, probable cause, or the driver's consent. The terrorist know that, and the latest such regulations have made the job of detecting bombs and or explosives, in the crowded places of the city, much more difficult.

It is amazing to see big city officials, trying to limit the gun violence with new laws and regulations that the criminal element would never obey. They don't get the notion that what is needed is not gun control, but criminal control. And when you see a city mayor, like Bill de Blasio, violating the very Constitution he swore to protect, you have to question the reasons for poor quality of life there, high taxes, and the flight of middle class to other states, constantly shrinking the tax basis, causing less people to have to pay much more for city services. Is that an indication of the "new normal" or a sign of a coming revolution, as engineered by the Democrat Marxists?

Some cities are just destined to bring back the old stone-age, when it comes to quality of life, even if their population rejects the political-economic route taken by their politicians. Stamping out crime, shall be their primary preoccupation, not gun control.

STOPPING THE GUN VIOLENCE

According to the 2010 census data, there are 310 million people in the USA, and that includes men, women and children and, of course some illegal immigrants. At the same time, there are some 300 million firearms in the hands of the civilians. Add to these figures, the government-owned firearms, in the hands of the law enforcement people, and those in military hands, and you will see why the gun culture in America is so solidly anchored in the national psyche.

The often cited need for gun control is a favorite subject of the opportunistic politicians who often forget that it is against the law of the law to interfere with the ownership of firearms by law-abiding citizens. However, that does not imply that the same politicians would not try to implement gun control, while they fail to see that what we need is "criminal control".

The volume of firearms in the society is, mathematically, inversely proportional to the crime level. More guns present in an area, less crime occurs, and in area where guns are prohibited, the crime index skyrockets. Cities like New York, Chicago, Detroit and Washington, DC, which have some of the most restrictive laws in the country, and exhibit also an unacceptable crime level.

The sociologists argue that the violence in United States of America will continue to remain unacceptably high, until the Congress will to institute extremely severe punishment, other than incarceration, for gun crimes, including the death penalty.

The current demographics of crime statistics, offer an image that is frighteningly bloody, because quite a large segment of the population had divorced from the elementary clauses of the social contract. Every individual is obligated to respect certain rules in order to belong to the society. The statistical data is revealing:

Racial Group	% of population	% of crimes
White	72.2 %	40.0 %
Black	12.6 %	28.0 %
Hispanic	8.0 %	22.0 %
Native American	5.0 %	7.0 %
Asiatic	2.0 %	2.0 %
Other	0.2 %	1.0 %

According to the FBI 2016 crime statistics consisting in felonies perpetrated against persons or property. Offenses which did not result in jail terms are not included. The total US population, per 2010 census, was 310,000,000 people.

The total number of criminal offenses in 2016 was some 6.5 million cases, which translate to 21 cases per 100,000 people, in terms of crimes against persons or property. Even though most police departments do not report violent crimes in relation to the ethnicity of the perpetrators, specific data regarding the race of the criminals is scrupulously collected, and many state statisticians try to decipher the meaning of that information.

One prime conclusion is that the Whites commit most crimes in the United States, followed, in order, by Blacks, and Hispanics.

However, relative to population composition, the Hispanics commit the most crimes, followed by the Blacks. The very high incidence of violent crime in the Hispanic communities could be attributed to the large number of illegal immigrants which includes a significant number of gang members "imported" from the Latin American countries of central and southern America.

In a study made by a group of doctoral candidates at the University of Chicago, in 2016, in which the gun violence in US was analyzed over the last three decades, the overwhelming conclusion was that the only solution could be offered by some extremely severe laws that would impose automatic death penalty for certain crimes:

Commission of crime using firearms;

Possession of guns by felons and gang members;

Possession of guns by illegal aliens and foreigners;

Drug importing and dealing;

All types of hate crimes, and

All acts of terrorism.

But that would be a move that most attorneys would oppose on account of "cruel and unusual punishment" depriving them of th he income they would make defending violent criminals.

POINTS TO PONDER

s we live in today, offer complex situations that no previous generation ever experienced, and in spite of all the technological advances, our lives did not get much better. We still have to work, to get a roof over our heads and meals on the table.

The today's criminals have sophisticated methods to steal and to hurt others, and we all have to be ready to escape safely unforeseen dangers, everywhere. The law enforcement people can't be everywhere, so we have to be mature enough to be able defend ourselves. The God's laws, the US Constitution, and common sense dictate that we do that, or else we may end up as numbers in statistical reports.

The only advantage we have, over previous generations is the availability of means to stand up against the criminal element. We have a large variety of means to insure our safety and survival. We may get the necessary training to handle guns, similarly to any good insurance policy, in the hope that we will never need to use it, knowing that it is infinitely better to have it, than to need it.

As most survival experts suggest, there are only three ways to act and prepare for handling emergencies:

Situational awareness, means that you need to know in detail what's around you, who may be a threat, and what exits you may have in case circumstances force you to act in your own defense;

Preparedness, means that you need to get all the training necessary to be able to properly handle a situation that requires a firearm, and to know when to use it, and when not;

Negotiation savvy, means that you are mature enough, to be able to avoid confrontations, and to talk your way out violence.

The oriental notion of "peaceful warrior", which offers the means to counter violence peacefully, was never more apt to try to synthesize the core principles of survival in a world full of criminal violence and total disregard for human life.

Unfortunately, the firearms are an integral part of this scene.

The controversial positions taken by various media outlets, and a certain group of politicians, regarding gun control, versus those who support the constitutional mandates immortalized by our Founding Fathers in the Constitution, are quite indicative of the lack of unitary thinking of our citizenry. We were never so deeply divided before in our way of thinking, as today.

Yet both factions those who propose draconic gun control measures, and those who oppose them, do have some valid points, which this small booklet tries to reveal from various perspectives.

The idea that armed security makes people less safe, is a total fallacy that our mass media spreads at nauseam.

The other aspect of this controversy is the thesis that the US Constitution entitles everyone to obtain and bear arms. Some people argue quite unreasonably, that the Constitution does not place any kind of limits on its applications of its amendments.

Such people argue that there is not a single mention in the US Constitution about people with disabling mental diseases, felons or criminals, since all the citizens are equal under the law. That is a deadly fallacy which did prove often that there is a need to impose some specific limits, in certain areas of law application.

The Congress, as the nation's legislative body, has the duty to see that any wide application of the people's civil rights would not result in harm to anyone.

The justification of some 15 Congressional Acts regulating firearms, ever since 1930s, was unable to stop the carnage caused by people with guns.

On the other hand, the argument that automobiles in USA do cause much more deaths than guns, and consequently, they have to be all banned, is also an artificial one.

Today's politicians seem not to care if their laws work or not. All they want is to pass more laws to limit the rights of the law-abiding citizens to obtain and bear arms. What they miss is to find out that no matter what kind of laws the Congress promulgates, the criminal would never respect any of them.

That illustrates the need to focus on criminals' control and not on gun control. Aside from any other legal considerations, one has to be aware of the fact that no one can insure morality, or the correct application of the law, by state or federal agencies. There will always be some cases in which the criminal element gets to operate "under the radar", or uses unforeseen loopholes in the text of the law, thanks to starving young attorneys.

The most prevalent opinions about gun control, vis-à-vis law enforcement, regards the fault of the justice system, which was converted to a "litigation industry", where ineffective judges place the citizenry at risk, through light sentences, which always favor the criminals. That is a situation that needs reconsideration!

In assessing the primary elements of gun violence, most of the official statistics neglect to focus on the psychology and the mental health of the perpetrators.

The first place in this classification belongs to adult males with good knowledge about firearms, gained during military service, or through sport shooting practice or hunting, but that does not imply, by any means, that such activities need to be banned.

The second group of gun violence criminals is formed by young or immature males, with serious psychiatric handicaps. Such criminals resemble a barrel with gunpowder waiting for a spark from static electricity charges.

The last group of criminals who produce horrible acts of gun violence, is formed of bandits of opportunity, who are enticed to act when they see conditions in which they do not face any king of possible retribution, such as a door forgotten unlocked or open, a car with the key in the ignition, with the motor running, or a house with no lights.

ANATOMY OF A HOME INVASION

When Yolanda Rousseau, of Kenner, Louisiana, turned onto the old street where her little house was, she noticed a group of four or five young men, but she did not pay too much attention to their presence. That was primarily a black neighborhood, and one or two young Black men in the street did not warrant additional scrutiny. She knew from her own experience, that many of the young Black men, are thieves of opportunity, naturally inclined to commit various acts, yet the 65-years-old grandmother was not too worried. Ever since she obtained her permit to carry a handgun, she kept her head high, determined to resist any kind of attempts to intimidate her, or to limit her freedom in the city that she loved. During the last ten years, or so, she had no reason to think that she would ever become a crime victim.

She parked her white 2014 Ford Focus in the driveway, on her usual spot, next to the one her daughter would park, checked the mail box, and entered her house with a handful of envelopes and magazines. Seated at the kitchen table, she scanned the mail just received, and got her shoes off, sighing with relief, when her feet enjoyed a little bit of freedom from confinement. Her only daughter, Nadine, was out of town for the next couple of days, being alone in the house, she turned on the TV, for company. It was shortly after 6:00 PM and the mews bulletin was talking about the sharp increase in the violent crime in the New Orleans area. She knew that a significant part of state of Louisiana was predominantly Democratic, and favored leftist causes, yet she was quite convinced that most Black people there, like herself, were conservative. She reasoned that: "If you work for your money, have a house for which you pay mortgage, go to church regularly, like sports, and own a hunting rifle, or a pistol, you are conservative, matter what others do or say."

Often, she'd talk with her daughter, Nadine, about the changes in peoples' attitudes that followed that Katrina hurricane, of August 2005, when the quality of life there took a severe dive.

It seems that only a handful, of the original Kenner old residents remained in her neighborhood, most being replaced by those who came from all over the creation, like from New York, Miami, Chicago, Memphis, or Atlanta. Louisiana has definitely lost her traditionally unhurried, peaceful life that anyone associated with the "speak easy" culture of the past. She missed that dearly.

Working in a local bank, she heard numerous stories about elderly people being robbed in plain daylight, or had their cars hijacked. That's why she applied for a concealed handgun permit, after spending a couple of weekends in a special training class. There she learned how to shoot, and how to differentiate between the situations which justify deadly force, and those which do not. While waiting for her license to carry a concealed gun, she was terrified by what happened, to one lady living probably less than four blocks away from her house. That case was broadcast as a news item one evening, and concerned a retired bank employee who applied for a concealed gun license, in view of the fact that local gangs often victimized the elderly. She was murdered in front of her own house, while waiting for the license that would have allowed her to defend herself with a gun, in such a situation.

Yolanda Rousseau did not want anything like that to happen to her. She religiously carried every day, wherever she went, her Beretta 9 mm pistol in her purse, in a little pouch, which on its outside, had a transparent pockets which displayed her makeup kit.

She gained a different demeanor after she obtained her concealed gun license. She kept her head up, never showed any kind of fear or hesitation, when some unsavory character crossed her path and acted provocatively. She was quite sure of herself, and the criminal element knew not to mess with little old ladies who did not show fear toward anyone who was thinking to snatch a purse.

It was shortly after 7:30 PM when her doorbell rang. She opened the door, and there were Bob and Pamela, two of her best friends, who, returning home from shopping dropped in, just to chat a little. Pleasantly surprised by that visit, she noticed a group of four teenagers on the other side of the street, but she did not pay additional attention to that scene, even if those youngsters seemed not to belong there. As she served her guests some peach cobbler and iced water, talking and laughing, the front door burst open and three youngsters got in wielding knives. The fourth individual did remain outside, probably as a look-out.

Bob jumped up in the defense of the two ladies and was stabbed in the chest. Yolanda bent down, picked her purse, and ironically asked:

"Do you want my money?"

"Give me your purse, you bitch!"

Yolanda reached in her purse withdrew her handgun, and fired two deadly shots. Two of the surviving tugs took off at an impressive speed. After calling the 911 and the ambulance medical emergency personnel stopped Bob's hemorrhage, they transported him to the emergency room. The police compiled a lengthy report, and took a lot of photographs of the scene, and of the cadavers of the two dead criminals, drawing sketches of Yolanda's house. They called the night judge who ruled the two homicides as justified. In the state of Louisiana deadly force is permitted in order to prevent any situations that may result in injury or death.

After verifying the identity of the two dead bandits, the local police found out that the two men were quite known to police, as having an extremely long criminal record, which included robbery, rape, grand theft, and car-jacking. They have been just released from the Angola prison, after serving five years for violent crimes. Their two accomplices were also found, and arrested by the local police.

A local TV station wanted to ask Yolanda Rousseau for an interview for their evening crime monitoring program, but she refused to do it. It was a very sad situation, she thought, that she needed to waste two young lives, but, on the other hand, her life was just as precious, and defending it, was a God-given right. After a couple of days spent in the hospital, following some surgery to fix a severed artery, Bob was allowed to go home, where he filed a state application for a concealed gun permit. His wife, Pamela did the same thing. Three weeks later they were in a classroom, studying the correct ways to behave with a gun.

The neighborhood homeowners association purchased and placed at both ends of her street some signs proclaiming in red letters:

> "This is not a gun free zone. All the criminals will be prosecuted to the full extent of the law, if they survive"

The police department liked those signs, and paid to have many of them placed in neighborhoods where criminal activities kept them busy, especially on weekends. What this initiative did quite well, was to push the hardened criminals out of the residential areas. However, that had a negative effect: the criminals moved to the malls and to the shopping centers, which had their own security force.

Home invasions occur even if even when there is no one home, like in the case of home burglaries, when people lose a lot of their possessions, usually accompanied by the heart-breaking damages caused by ransacking criminals.

The FBI's most recent public data shows that over $3.9 billion was lost due to burglaries in 2014. That simply means that the average burglary victim loses at least $ 2,500 when that happens. And most victims lose much more than that, if you count irreplaceable items with sentimental value. You'd need to make sure that your home is never broken into and you never lose a single penny, or have to deal with the terrors of a home invasion. In America huge corporations like Brinks, ADT, and the other big security companies, have fed us consistently a line of B.S. over the last few decades. You've seen their commercials, that go something like this:

"Did you know a burglary happens every 20 seconds in the U.S.? Well if you install our fancy alarm system you'll never have to worry about being robbed, and even better, you'll get a discount on your homeowners insurance!"

    These are multi-billion dollar corporations and they spend tens of millions every year running TV ads, Radio ads, sending salesmen door to door, and every other form of marketing you can imagine, and we buy into it, hook, line and sinker. They offer "free installation and free equipment" if you'll just sign up for their monthly monitoring plans. Then you pay them every month, for the rest of your life to have them "monitor" your house. And what do you get out of it? A large dog would be your best alarm. When a stranger forces his or her way into your house, at night, resist the urge to turn the lights on. You know the inside of your home in the dark, while the burglars or the invaders, do not. That is your tactical advantage.

    If you are proficient with a gun, use it. But if it sits in your nightstand, and you never used it, you should run rather than fire it. The last thing you need in such an emergency is to shoot a couple of rounds through the walls of your home.

WOMEN AND GUNS

The relatively popular misconception that only the men are "good with guns", is a sexist fallacy, which ignores the thousands of ladies, who are a part of our country's military, law enforcement, and of the shooting sports enthusiasts.

A 25-years old beauty queen, in Florida, Meghan Brown, was suddenly awaken, in the middle of the night, in her Tierra Verde home, by someone breaking her back door and forcing his way in.

Confronting the intruder, she was knocked to the floor, dragged by her hair, and suffered head and face injuries from the criminal's kicks. Her fiancé, awaken also by the noise, jumped to defend her.

That caused the intruder to turn away from Meghan, and she took the opportunity to retrieve a handgun from a drawer, after which she fired two shots, killing the home invader.

The bandit, the 42-years-old Albert Franklin Hill, it turned out, after the police arrived, to be a habitual criminal with a lengthy criminal record, which included rapes, grand theft, robberies, and manslaughter. He was just released from prison one week earlier, after he served eight years out of a sentence of twelve years. The County Attorney found that homicide justified, as a bona-fide self-defense act, and no charges were ever filed against Meghan Brown, or her fiancé. That was one of the many cases that occur daily, in which a law-abiding citizen had to use a gun to survive a criminal's attack, and no reasonable mind would argue against this use of firearms.

Another example of criminals using guns, while law-abiding citizen were sitting ducks, is offered by the Luby's massacre. The Luby's shooting took place on October 16, 1991, at a Luby's Cafeteris, in Killeen, Texas,

The perpetrator, George Hennard, 35, drove his blue Ford Ranger pickup truck through the front window of the restaurant, after which he rapidly shot and killed 23 people, and wounded 27 others. He had a brief shootout with the police, and refused to obey their orders to surrender, and, finally, he fatally shot himself in the head.

Ranked, at the time, as the deadliest mass shooting in Texas, its death toll was only surpassed by that of the VA Tech mass shooting of April 2007. As of February 2018, this incident ranked as the sixth-deadliest shooting in the US by a single shooter.

It was National Boss's Day, and the Luby's cafeteria was crowded to full capacity. At first, bystanders thought the crash of that truck was just an accident, but after Hennard started shooting, some patrons tried to escape from the cafeteria, almost immediately. The first victim was a veteri-narian, Dr. Michael Griffith. Another patron, one Tommy Vaughn, threw himself through a rear window, sustaining multiple injuries, but thus he created an escape avenue, for himself and for some 50 other cafeteria patrons. Hennard was described by the few people who knew him, as reclusive and belligerent, with an explosive temper.

He had been kicked out of the Merchant Marine because of his possession and use of marijuana and other drugs on the job. Numerous reports included a few accounts of Hennard's expressed extreme hatred for women, which included his own mother. An ex-roommate of his said that:

"He hated Blacks, Hispanics, gays, and married people. He believed that all women were snakes, and always had few derogatory remarks about them, especially after fights with his mother".

Some survivors of that cafeteria shootings said that Hennard had passed over men, to shoot only women. 14 of the 23 people killed were women, as were many of the wounded. He called some of them "vipers", "bitches" and "whores", before he did shoot them to death.

The Glock C-17, 9 mm, and the Rugger P-8, 9 mm pistols which Hennard used to kill Luby's patrons, were all legally purchased, during February or March 1991 at a gun shop in Henderson, NV.

One of the Luby's customers, on that tragic day, was a Texas chiropractor, Dr. Suzanna Gratia Hupp, who was having a meal with her parents, when the small blue pickup truck burst through the cafeteria's front glass plates.

The irony of those circumstances consists in the fact that Dr. Hupp always did carry a handgun in her purse, but this time, apprehensive of falling on the wrong side of the Texas law, she locked it in the trunk of her car, a decision that she regretted for the rest of her life.

In response to the trauma of losing both her parents to a criminal act, she became a vocal activist for adopting a law that would allow concealed weapons in Texas.

Incidentally, exactly at the same time, an anti-crime bill was scheduled for a vote in the US House of Representatives, just one day after the Luby's massacre.

Some of the Hennard's victims had been constituents of Representative Chet Edwards, and in response, he abandoned his opposition to a gun control provision that was part of that bill. The provision, which did not pass, would have banned some weapons and magazines like the ones used by Hennard.

The NRA, Texas State Rifle Association, and others preferred that the state allows its citizens to carry concealed handguns, with full support from Dr. Hupp, now an elected member to the Texas House of Representatives.

The Democratic Texas governor, Ann Richards, vetoed that bill, but in 1995, her Republican successor, George W. Bush, signed the concealed carry law in Texas. Dr. Suzanna Hupp, who survived Luby's shooting, worked hard to get elected to the Texas House of Representatives, so that she could initiate the passing of the concealed gun carry law. She later testified that she would have liked to have had her gun, but said, "It was a hundred feet away, in my car" (she had feared that if she was caught carrying it, she might lose her chiropractor's license). She testified across the country in support of concealed handgun laws, and was elected to the Texas House of Representatives for five consecutive terms starting in in 1996.

She wrote a best-seller, "From Luby's to the State Legislature: One Woman's Fight Against Gun Control" which was published by the Privateer Publications of San Antonio, Texas.

Dr. Hupp has been often quoted in such publications, as US News & World Report, the Wall Street Journal, Texas Monthly, Time, New York Times, People Magazine, and many others, in addition to being featured on several TV news programs, like the 48 Hours, World News Tonight, and 60 Minutes. What a lady!

We all have mothers, wives, and daughters, and we all consider family safety a matter of national security! Is there anyone, who thinks that women still can't measure up to men's "standards", when it comes to determination in face of the dangers thrust upon them by the criminal element?

If that's the case, the author suggests that such a person shall get out of the ancestral cave, and look around. The sun does not move around the earth and the earth is not flat.

It is quite hard to believe that there are still people who do not accept fundamental truths, because of superstitious placed in their mind by lack of education, and a sickly attitude driven by a fallacious sexist need to be always on top, vis-a-vis the women who shall all be in an inferior position.

CHILDREN AND GUNS

Children, through their natural curiosity, are attracted to guns, and the adults, including their parents, have to be aware of this. Even though, from a legal stand point, children are not considered of reason age below 12-years of age, a lot of tragedies happen when a boy or a girl touches a firearm.

Boys, by their own physiological nature, are always more inclined to become belligerent and aggressive in their relations with other children. Girls, on the other hand, have a tendency to be more peaceful, with some exceptions. We all saw lately however, the savage fights between teenager girls on the Youtube, when they pull each other by hair, scratch their faces, and use deadly weapons. Just one generation ago that did not happen.

The youngest child, ever to kill someone with a gun, was a 5-years-old boy in Tennessee, who got hold of the gun his father kept in a night stand drawer, and shot his three-years-old sister. That was not an accident but a crass act of parental negligence from the part of the parents.

Frequently the parents cause tragedies by allowing their children to have access, willingly or not, to firearms. Our juvenile justice system keeps minor offenders shielded, by not revealing their identities, for "protection". Against what? That's why youngsters accumulate criminal records that can rival seasoned gangsters, and by the time they mature to adulthood, no one knows that, because the US juvenile court systems will keep all such records sealed.

Add to the image of unruly children the lack of proper guidance in our public schools, the Hollywood influence in violent movies, and videogames, and you will see why the outlook on the actions to curb violence in our society seem to be dark. Today's children form the characteristics of the future society, which in our case seems to continue to keep the gun violence as a guarantee for the next tragedies.

In a suburban school, in an affluent Philadelphia area, when the children were asked what they wanted to be, some 25% of them answered with "drug dealers". No one wanted to become policeman, firefighter, pilot, or sea captain, as it was the case just two generations ago. That is a clear sign of the severity of the disconnection between the real life of our youngsters, and the needs of the society.

To blame only the parents, or the school systems, would be awfully unfair, because neither the parents, nor the schools operate in a vacuum, as shielded from the political pressures. All the tax revenue issues, cut into the quality of life, more so in poor immigrant communities, where gang activities are the only extra-curricular activity that keeps children busy. The allure of easy money is quite a powerful motivator which cannot compete with the rigors of a day-to-day job that earlier generations considered normal.

Illegal activities, which often have as a corollary the gun violence, attract and captivate children older than 12.

They make excellent "drug runners", who, if caught, do not suffer any repercussions since juvenile court judges will let them back into society, because lack of space. They will only lock up extremely violent young criminals, who become a sore thumb in the juvenile justice system. The rest of the offenders, who do not present an acute danger to the local immediate community, remain free to improve their "skills".

A juvenile delinquent, in the United States, is a person who is typically below 18 years of age, (17 in New York, Missouri, North Carolina, New Hampshire and Texas), an act that otherwise would have been charged as a crime, if they were adults. Depending on the type and severity of the offense committed, it is possible for people under 18 to be charged and treated as adults, frequently under the threat of the death penalty.

In recent years, a much higher proportion of youth have experienced more arrests by their early 20s, than in the past, and some scholars have concluded that this is a reflection of a more aggressive criminal justice and zero-tolerance policies, rather than changes in youth attitude toward minor offenses, such as underage smoking or drinking,

According to federal statistics, the youth violence rates in the United States have dropped to approximately 12% of their peak rates reached in 1993. US government officials suggest that most juvenile offending is of non-violent nature.

This is justified by the fact that most teens tend to offend by committing non-violent crimes, only once or a few times, and only during adolescence. Repeated or violent acts are most likely to lead later to more violent offenses. When this happens, the offenders often display antisocial behavior, even before reaching adolescence.

Juvenile delinquency can be separated into three categories:

Delinquency or crimes committed by minors, which are dealt with in the juvenile courts of the justice system;

Criminal behavior, crimes dealt with by the criminal justice system;

Status offenses, that are thus classified as such, only because the offender is a minor, such as truancy, smoking, or drinking, are also dealt with by the juvenile courts.

According to the developmental research performed in 2016 by the University of Chicago, there are two different types of offenders that emerge in adolescence. One is the repeat offender, referred to as the life-course-persistent type of offender, who begins offending or showing antisocial or aggressive behavior in adolescence (or even in the early childhood), and continues well into adulthood, and the type of age-specific offenses, referred to as the adolescence-limited offenses, for whom juvenile offending or delinquency begins and ends during their period of adolescence.

Not all types of offenses place the seeds of gun violence in the hands of older adolescents. Young children, especially in minority areas of larger cities, like Los Angeles, Chicago, Philadelphia, New York, Houston or Miami, have been seen to kill remorselessly other children or adults, in the process of committing "adult crimes".

Juvenile delinquency occurrences by males are largely disproportionate to the rate of those committed by females. This huge gap between these crimes reinforces the customary connotation of traditional masculinity to be the center of most violence, aggression, and competition. This is largely based on the assumption that the males, take what they feel they deserve through these means, they define themselves and play the role of provider and independent clan figures. These societal conditions are cultivated by male peers, asserting the notion that most of the psychological symptoms described as pathological, are an ideal self-regulation devices imposed upon individuals to mimic the actions of role models of the male delinquents.

However, most of these delinquencies are rarely found in females, because the females are expected to be more docile individuals, and rely solely on dependent characters, shielding them from the need of committing delinquencies. Because aggression is not a desired type of characteristic in females, it has caused more commotion in young people's groups when females performed crimes that are most often attributed to males.

In 2015, some 79,800 juveniles were incarcerated in youth detention facilities alone. Approximately 500,000 youth are brought to detention centers in any given year.

This data does not reflect the juveniles tried as adults. Around 40% of them were incarcerated in privatized jails which are set up as for-profit facilities.

Only some 35% of the offenders are females, within a preponderance of minorities, like Blacks, Hispanics and Orientals.

The system that is currently operating in the United States was created under the 1974 law of Juvenile Justice and Delinquency Prevention Act, which called for an action of "deinstitutionalization" of the juvenile delinquents, under the assumption that this would reduce violent crime.

The act required that states holding youth within adult prisons for status offenses remove them within a span of two years (this timeframe was adjusted over time). The act also provided many program grants to states, based on their youth populations, and created the Office of Juvenile Justice and Delinquency Prevention, (OJJDP), which proves once more that throwing taxpayer money at a problem does not make it disappear. The violent crime, especially murders by firearms, continued to escalate, reaching an all-time high in 2015.

CHRISTIANITY AND GUNS

The Bible, in both texts of the Old Testament and in the New Testament present some precise indication about the God-given right to self-defense. That includes all aspects of defending one's family and possessions.

Some of Christ's disciples carried weapons as a normal safety and self-defense measure. Jesus' inner circle did not avoid swords or knives, as dangerous, or taboo. We find that in the texts of Luke 22:35-38, Jesus asked about the swords two of his apostles carried. The conclusion was that the weapons were not prohibited in the early Christian society, and that continued through all the centuries that followed, until our days.

Until the 1960s America never lost a war and had a relatively small standing military force, deemed sufficient to insure the US peace and defense. Between the wars, the US maintained a very small military force, compared to its total population.

The people relied on God, a small military, an armed police, and a civilian militia, and it worked well, for more than 200 years.

In Deuteronomy the Israelites were told by their kings, not to "rely too much on war horses", translating that to today's military mechanized units. As a good citizenry practice, the Christians were instructed to respect and obey armed policemen in the service of a free nation. Under conditions of tyranny and despotism, the thirst for freedom was understood to be favored and helped by God.

Romans 13:1 states clearly that we shall "Let every soul be subject unto the higher powers of God, for there is no power but that of God, and all the powers to be, are ordained by God. Thus he who whatsoever resisted the power, resisted the ordinance of God, and he who resisted it, shall receive damnation, for the rulers are not a terror to good works, but to evil. Thus thou shall not be afraid of the power, but do that which is good, and thou shall have all the praise."

Paul precisely affirmed that, one who detested the powers of the government he detested the ordinance of God. Placing that text in proper historical perspective, under the view of the Roman Empire's conquests, when Christian were persecuted savagely, one can see the early Christians' drive for peace and tranquility. That took another 300 years, to be accomplished, under Constantine the Great.

Jesus admonished his disciples, that if one slap us physically or verbally, we shall fight that with kindness. But that does not mean, that if an aggressor goes behind words, we shall remain passive. We have the right to defend ourselves, our family and our possession. Being too weak and passive encourages violence, and that is more relevant in our modern times. Our Founding Fathers wanted a strong society, armed, and safe from internal or external enemies.

Anyone who does not feel comfortable with a firearm, or is afraid of children harming themselves by finding a weapon, should feel no obligation to own one. We shall, all, rely deeply on God.

ISLAMISM AND GUNS

Islamism is a concept whose meaning has been debated in both public and academic circles. This term can refer to diverse forms of social and political activism advocating that public and political life should be guided by Islamic principles or in some cases by movements which call for full implementation of Sharia Law. It is commonly used interchangeably with the terms political Islam or Islamic fundamentalism. In Western media usage, that term tends to refer to groups who aim to establish a sharia-based Islamic state, often with the implication of violent tactics, and many human rights violations. That has acquired the connotations of maximum political extremism. In the Muslim world, the term has a positive meaning among its proponents.

Different currents of Islamist thought include advocating a "revolutionary" strategy of Islamizing the society through exercise in state power, and alternately a "reformist" strategy to continue the Islamizing process of the society through grass-roots social and political activism. Islamists may emphasize the implementation of Sharia Law, pan-Islamic political unity, including an Islamic state or selective removal of non-Muslims, particularly western people through direct action, in military, economic, political, social, and cultural fields, for the elimination of all influences in the Muslim world that they believe to be incompatible with the "pure" Islam.

Most Islamist thinkers emphasize the peaceful political processes, which are supported by the majority of contemporary Islamists however, peaceful means are rarely used to re-conquer the vast territories lost in Europe, Africa, and Asia, during the last centuries.

Prophet Mohammed, (570-632),who established Islam during the seventh century, was considered God's messenger, sent to the Arabs to confirm the mono-theistic teachings preached previously by Adam, Abraham, Moses Jesus and other prophets. The folklore has it that around the year 610 he started to preach about his own revelations, and he went to Jerusalem with a commercial caravan of camels, where he asked the Rabbinate of Judea, to be included in the Old Testament, as a prophet. The Jews laughed at him, and suggested that he takes a long walk, at night, through the desert, to clear his mind. Furious, he returned to Medina, where he murdered all the Jews he could catch. That hatred toward the Jews became the mark of Islam, and it manifests even todat.

In 619 Mohammed proclaimed forcefully that "God is One", and a complete and only a total surrender, ("Islaam"), to him, is the only right course of action that would take you into the Heaven.

The apologists who argued that Mohammed was an astute politician, a brilliant statesman, a great judge of character, a superb diplomat, and above all, a great military strategist, fail to observe that he was also capable of utter deception. He annihilated all the tribes which did not accept his drive to exterminate all the people who did not accept his leadership. Mohamed achieved total control of the Arabic tribes through the force of his swords, by using the so-called "Jihad", which determined convinced Muslims to murder all non-believers in selfish acts of sacrifice for Allah. And that act could not be achieved without weapons.

That's why the Muslims have been divided into two classes: Arabs, and non-Arabs. The Arabs are destined to be the rulers, and the non-Arabs have to be ruled for the glory of Allah. It took the Muslim less than 600 years to progress from sword and arrows, to firearms powered by gun powder.

It was during the 14th century that the pistols and muskets did become ubiquitous in the hands of the Muslim armies. That's why no self-respecting Muslim male would appear in public without his dagger and one or two pistols.

The presence of guns was imposed by the cultural necessity to appear powerful, unyielding, to non-believers. There were only a handful of restrictions in owning and using firearms. The non-Muslims were not allowed to display guns, like the slaves and the servants, who were stopped from acquiring guns, and there was a strong opposition to the idea of entering a mosque with weapons. Other than that the life in all the Muslim countries was a cheap commodity, which created a marked necessity to maintain very high birth rates. Sons were the preferred offspring, while for the females, the conquering armies of the Arab emirates or caliphates, would kidnap young females to reward warriors with them. That insured population growth. Thus the pairing of the gun culture with the taste for pillaging the communities of conquered people, did create a predilection for violence, that no Islamic scholar ever tried to temper down. As a result, most of the Muslim communities are quite violent everywhere, in Europe, Asia, Africa and in the US. The sad fact about this aspect of the Islamic culture is that more Muslims die from Muslims' bullets than from any other causes. Some scholarly works analyzing the animosity, between Shia and Sunni Muslims, consider the gun violence, and Islam, as totally inseparable.

The conclusion that Islam was never a religion, but only an offensive ideology, gains every day more popularity, fact which justifies an emerging reform movement in the Islamist circles.

Islamist theoreticians affirm that murder, suicide and homosexuality are all unpardonable sins, according to the Qur'an. Murder is not allowed by the Ten Commandments, which the Muslims do profess to respect, while the suicide is considered equivalent to murder. Tell that to the jihad suicide bombers! The intercourse between two men is also taken by the Qur'an, as a mortal sin, "shaking the throne of Allah."

But the Koran is mute about the sex with young boys. That's why Turkish Ottoman clerics ruled in 1400s that such sex acts are allowable, legislating rampant promiscuity.

Thus the issue of gun violence in Muslim the societies can measure almost to par with the violence visited upon other races or societies, by colonial powers.

Some verses from the Qur'an, like those found in 47:4 would provide an edifying example of violence in the Muslim society:

"When you see a non-believer, cut his head off."

CRIME CONTROL

All sort of politicians, media "specialists", and social engineers, good-intentioned people, or some not so good-intentioned, fan the issue of gun control, as a mean to curb gun violence. No matter what you think, you have to see that most of them "bark to the wrong tree",

Instead of proposing new laws for gun control, while the laws already existing are not enforced, they should focus harder on crime control. Gun violence does not happen in a vacuum, but in an environment which allows crime to thrive, as an industry for illicit profits. Closing down crime enterprises can do much more than the sterile philosophical debates on gun control.

Examine, for a moment, the most recent crime statistics compiled by various law enforcement agencies:

In 2017 Chicago had 2,987 gun-related injuries and 995 homicides, making it the murder capital of the US, followed by Detroit, with 1,975 gun-related injuries, and 593 deaths. By comparison, during the same period, New York City did record 1,421 gun related injuries and 395 homicides.

Los Angeles and the state of Maryland had also, high gun-related fatalities, but could not unseat Chicago for the first place.

It is quite interesting to see that the crime statistics are the highest in cities run by Democrat administrations, yet in New York City, the crime rate decreased considerably from 1994 to 2014. In

1994 when Rudy Giuliani became mayor, a massive effort was undertaken to reduce the crime rate, and to improve the life of that city's dwellers.

In 1996, during his first term as mayor of the New York City, based on the legal precedent of the Terry v. Ohio case of 1968, the city police was empowered to use "Terry Stops".

That name is derived from the case in which the USA Supreme Court held that police may briefly detain a person whom they reasonably suspect is involved in some criminal activity. The Supreme Court also held that police may do a limited search of the suspect's outer garments for weapons, if they have a "reasonable or an articulable suspicion that the person detained, may be armed and dangerous." That was the basis of "stop and Frisk" acts.

To have reasonable suspicion that would justify a stop, police must be able to point to "specific and articulable facts" that would indicate to a reasonable police officer that the man stopped, is or is about to be engaged in some sort of criminal activity, as opposed to proof of past conduct. Reasonable suspicion depends on the "totality of circumstances", and it can result from a combination of facts, each of which may, by itself, be totally innocuous. The "Terry Stops", also called "Giuliani's Cleanup" in New York, removed, during the first year, over 2,900 firearms out of the hands of dangerous felons, who were placed back in prison, since they were prohibited from owning any guns.

Several other major cities did try to emulate the New York's example, with excellent results, except for Chicago, Detroit and

Washington, DC. Consequently, the crime rate in the Big Apple dropped by more than 45%, for the first time since 1940. Rudi Giuliani was the mayor of New York City between 1994 and 2001, and was succeeded by Michael Blumberg, who tried to maintain the status quo, without ever trying to "rock the boat". The next mayor, Bill de Blasio, who was elected in 2014, blamed falsely the increase in city violent crime, on previous administrations. He set out to prove that the gun violence in the city of New York is due to illegally obtained firearms from out of state venues.

To prove his point, he selected three retired policemen to act as private detectives, and sent them to Arizona and Texas, to try to demonstrate how easy it is to obtain illegal guns.

In Arizona they went to the "Crossroads of the West" Gun Show in Phoenix, where no gun dealer would sell them any kind of firearms, with their New York identification papers, that they could not tell if they were valid or not.

Next, they went to the "Wild Weasel" Gun Show, in the town of Kingsland, Texas, where they attempted to purchase some ten firearms. The dealers there, refused categorically to sell anything to those "suspiciously looking New York guys". Mayor's Bill de Blasio experiment turned out to be a $100,000 failure that the New York taxpayers could have gladly missed to foot the bill for.

The last mayor of the New York City, in 2018, seemed much more preoccupied with the comfort of the illegal immigrants and of the welfare of the criminals, by declaring that city, a "sanctuary city" while the "Terry Stops" have been totally discontinued, on account of possible civil right violations, even though the US Supreme Court set up exact parameters for their implementation.

Under the constraints of several legal precedents, the police may randomly search vehicles, under the "plain view doctrine", and can seize and use as evidence, weapons or contraband visible from outside the vehicle. The New York City legal staff urged the local law enforcement personnel to avoid doing that without a warrant, a probable cause, or the driver's consent. The terrorist know that, and the latest such regulations have made the job of detecting bombs, and or explosives, in the crowded places of the city, much more difficult.

It is amazing to see big city officials, trying to limit the gun violence with new laws and regulations that the criminal element would never obey. They rarely get the notion that what is needed is not gun control, but criminal control. And when you see a city mayor, like Bill de Blasio, violating the very Constitution he swore to protect, you do not have to question the reasons for poor quality of life there, high taxes, and the flight of middle class to other states, constantly shrinking the tax basis, causing less people to have to pay much more in taxes, for city services.

Is that an indication of the "new normal", or a severe sign of a coming revolution, as engineered by the leftists?

The ebb and flow of public attitudes will soon change again, in the favor of logic and common sense.

STOPPING THE GUN VIOLENCE

According to the 2010 census data, there are now 310 million people in the USA, and that includes men, women, children and, of course, some illegal immigrants. At the same time, there are over 300 million firearms in the hands of the civilians. Add to these figures, the government-owned firearms, in the inventory of the law enforcement people, plus those in the military, and you will see why the gun culture in America is so solidly anchored in the national psyche.

Of the total number of 2.79 million deaths in 2015, of any and all causes, some over 100,000 occurred in the health care environment, due to misdiagnosis, wrong medication, or due to pathogens found in hospital air.

Next, in the order of magnitude, are some 40,000 deaths due to traffic accidents. The deaths caused by firearms only account for some 13,266 cases, while 1,200, or so deaths have been attributed to natural disasters. Compared to the 22 other high-income nations the U.S. gun-related murder rate is 25 times higher. Although it has half the population of all the other 22 nations combined, the U.S. had 82 percent of all gun deaths, 90 percent of all women killed with guns, 92 percent of children under 14, and 90 percent of all the young people between ages 15 and 20, killed with guns. In 2015, gun violence cost U.S. taxpayers approximately $516 million in direct hospital cost, plus the loss of time from work.

The gun violence is most common in poor urban areas and

it is frequently associated with gang violence, often involving male juveniles, or young adult males. Although the mass shootings have been covered extensively in the media, mass shootings in the USA, account for only a small fraction of gun-related deaths, and the frequency of such events declined steadily between 1994 and 2007, rising sharply only between 2007 and 2015. (In areas ruled by new Democratic administrations)

Legislative efforts at the federal, state, and local levels have attempted to address gun violence issues through a variety of new methods, including restricting firearms purchases by youth and other "at-risk" populations, setting waiting periods for firearm purchases, establishing gun buyback programs, law enforcement and policing strategies, stiff sentencing of gun law violators, more educational programs for parents and children, and community-outreach actions. Despite the widespread concerns about the high impact of gun violence on public health, the US Congress has prohibited the Centers for Disease Control, (CDC), from collecting any new research data, that could fall in the favor of gun control. The CDC has interpreted this ban to extend to all research on gun violence prevention, and because of that, it has not funded any kind of research on this subject, since 1996.

In 2015, some studies, including those undertaken by special congressional committees, showed that in the USA there were approximately 65 million gun owners. These legal firearm owners possessed approximately 300 million firearms, of which only an estimated 105 million of them were handguns.

The effectiveness and safety of guns used for personal use in defense, is debated. Studies place the instances of guns used for personal defense to a level as low as 65,000 times per year, and as high as 1.5 million times per year.

Under President Clinton's, administration the Department of Justice conducted a survey in 1994, that placed the frequency of guns used in personal defense at 1.5 million times per year, but noted that this was most likely an overestimate.

Eleven years later, in 2015, under President Barack Obama's administration, the rates mentioned above, more than doubled. The explanation of that increase is debatable, as government official claimed insufficient statistical information.

Some specialists argued that if all the specific data would have been compiled properly the statistics would look some three times higher, affirming, tongue in chick, that Barack Obama was the best salesman the firearm industry ever had.

In 2015, Arizona State University researcher, Sherry Towers, came to the conclusion that the:

> "National news media attention is like a 'vector' that reaches people who are vulnerable by becoming instant copycats."

She stated that disaffected people can become infected by the attention given other disturbed people who have thus become mass killers. She faults the Hollywood productions, as an element which contributes to the glorification of violence, stating that nothing will change until the Congress curbs the freedom of speech which incites to violence.

Another study, by the University of Chicago, focused in 2015 on the composition of the victims of gun violence, and pointed out to the fact the African Americans were 55% of the victims of gun homicides but only 13% of the total population of the US. Whites represented some 25% of victims but over 65% of the total number. Hispanics were 17% of victims and only some 16% of the US population. According to the U.S. Bureau of Justice Statistics, from 2000 to 2010, 24% of White homicide victims were killed by Whites, and 95% of Black homicide victims were killed by Blacks.

Public policy, as related to preventing gun violence, is an ongoing political and social debate, regarding both the restriction and availability of firearms within the United States. The policy at the Federal level has been governed by several legal instruments among the principal ones include:

Second Amendment,

National Firearms Act of 1934,

Gun Control Act of 1968,

Firearm Owners Protection Act of 1986,

Brady Handgun Violence Prevention Act of 1993,

Violent Crime Control and Law Enforcement Act of 1994,

Domestic Violence Offender Act Gun Ban of 1996.

Gun policies in the U.S. have been revised many times with acts such as those mention above, proving that there are scores of laws dealing with gun use in the commission of any criminal acts, underlying a position taken by gun advocates, which sustain that what is needed is not gun control, but criminal control.

Any logically-thinking individual would agree 100% with this opinion.

Violence prevention, and education are the key to curb gun violence. Specialized educational programs aimed to change the personal behavior of both children, and their parents, encouraging children to stay away from guns, ensuring that the parents store guns safely, and it encourages children to solve disputes without resorting to violence. Some of the most worthwhile examples come from the various states where the incidence of gun violence is on a decline, like in New Mexico, Arkansas, and Oklahoma.

The primary factor in detecting local causes of gun deaths would be a study of family life. In almost all the larger cities, the family life is shortchanged by single parents who try to raise their dysfunctional children alone. The most severe factor in the picture of violent children is the absence of a father figure. That fact is even more important for young boys who never knew a father in their lives. That makes them easy prey to the lethal attraction of gang lawlessness, crime, and the illicit drug money.

The only male models they interact with are the big-time drug dealers, who sport all the signs of affluence, from attire to luxury cars, for which the minors "run errands". The truth of the matter is that the total collapse of the family, as the basic social institution, occurs most frequently in association with the poor minority segments of the population victimized by the cultivation of the predatory instincts of the young gangsters.

The Hollywood productions have lost their educative content by thriving solely on "bullets, blood, and guts".

Add to this the extremely violent video games, and you will see that any attempt to turn around the current generation is just a wishful idea, that do-gooders try to fit somehow into the current social landscape. Is that a lost cause?

There are thousands of TV or Hollywood movies which are based solely on mayhem and bloody scenes, peppered with bullets from fully automatic weapons, torture, and death. What that does to a young mind is easily seen from the way the children play, and in the references they make to characters from some violent video games.

By the time a child reaches the age of 10, he may have seen on the TV more than 1,000 violent crimes, has seen some of the cartoon characters shot to death, only to reappear in the next video scene, removing any thought regarding the permanency of death.

Growing accustomed to the effects of violence becomes like a second nature. They lack compassion, they lack any kind of consideration for other children, and grow rebellious, and that becomes like a social cancer. Most of the time any kind of early corrective intervention is simply impossible, by being too late.

Many children end up shot to death by police, by brandishing toy guns in a threatening manner, or by staging holdups with toy guns, that had their reflective bands, required by law, removed to resemble real guns. And that is, also, the result of the gun culture.

GUN SAFETY

The only gun safety programs aimed to youngsters, that can demonstrate a good level of success, are offered by associations and clubs like those sponsored by the NRA, and few others.

By contrast, the programs implemented, by various branches of the state or federal governments, geared towards children, have not been successful at all. The many inherent challenges which will arise when working with children, include their tendency to perceive themselves as invulnerable, showing a very limited ability to apply lessons learned, and by immature curiosity, under peer pressure.

The goal of most gun safety programs, usually administered by local firearms dealers, and by shooting clubs, is to teach older children and adolescents how to handle firearms safely. There has been no systematic evaluation of the effect of such programs on children. For adults, no positive effect on gun storage practices has been found, as a result of these programs. Also, researchers have discovered that gun safety programs for children may, most likely, increase a child's interest in obtaining and using guns, which they cannot be expected to use safely, due to inherent immaturity.

One approach taken is gun avoidance, such as when a child encounters a firearm at a neighbor's home. The Edward Eagle, a Gun Safety Program, administrator for the NRA, is geared toward younger children from the first grade to the sixth, and teaches kids that real guns are not toys, by emphasizing a "just say no" stance, when offered to "play" with guns. Edward Eagle program is based on training children in a four-step action mandatorily needed to be taken when children see a firearm:

(1) Stop! (2) Don't touch! (3) Leave the area! (4) Go tell an adult!

Sociologists and psychologists agree that to determine inner-city youths not to carry guns "requires convincing them that they can survive in their neighborhood without being armed, that they can come and go in peace, that being unarmed will not cause them to be victimized, intimidated, or slain", but that does not ring true in many large cities. Intervention programs, such as the Cease Fire Chicago, Boston, Philadelphia, during the 1980s and the, Project Exile, in Richmond, VA during the 1990s, have been shown to be somewhat effective. Other intervention strategies, such as gun "buy-back" programs, have demonstrated to be totally ineffective.

Americans for Responsible Solutions was started in January 2013 as a non-profit organization whose mission is to:

"Encourage elected officials to stand up to find solutions to prevent gun violence, and also to protect the responsible gun owners, by communicating directly with the constituents that elected them."

The organization was announced on January 8, 2013 by Gabrielle Gifford, a former Democratic member of the US House of Representatives, and Mark Kelly, her husband, now a retired American astronaut. In an editorial published in USA Today, Gifford and Kelly approached to the NRA lobby and sought to counter it by creating a different movement dedicated solely to responsible gun control practices.

The process of research into firearms and violent crime is quite difficult, due to limited data on gun ownership, and due to the use of subjective market data. The studies into gun violence have primarily taken one of two approaches:

1) Case history studies, and

2) Social-psychological studies of gun violence.

Gun ownership data is usually obtained through some public surveys, market reports, and sometimes, from production data of import, and sales figures, from the domestic distribution channels. That usually results in some questionable conclusions, since the beneficiaries of those studies, who foot the bills, are not a neutral party, being only driven by the business' bottom line.

Tabulating all the elements of the cases studied through the police reports, can offer a realistic image of the occurrence of the gun violence. Breaking down further that data, the inescapable conclusion is that the urban areas are considerably more dangerous than the rural environment. Practically, there are no cases of gun violence perpetrated by children in rural areas. That is due, most likely due to the more stable family life around farms and ranches, and due to wide participation in church activities.

The social-psychology studies reveal that, by far, the greatest majority of children that commit violent acts with guns come from broken families, without a father. Many of the children studied, never ever went to church while most of their mothers, as single parents, had to work more than one job, leaving their children without any kind of supervision for the largest part of the day and evening. It is realistic to assume that such children are practically only street-educated, and the results of that education can be seen in the police blotters, and in the Juvenile Courts.

This infamous situation will continue to persist, as long as the people in authority do not accept the fact that stopping the children gun violence is a matter of national security.

GUN RUNNING

Gun running is the trafficking of contraband weapons and ammunition. What constitutes legal trade in firearms varies widely, depending on local and national laws.

The 1999 Report of the UN Panel of Governmental Experts on Small Arms, provides a more refined and precise definition, which has become internationally accepted. This distinguishes between small arms (revolvers and self-loading pistols, rifles and carbines, submachine guns, assault rifles, and light machine guns) which are weapons designed for personal use, and heavy weapons (heavy machine guns, hand-held under-barrel, and truck-mounted grenade launchers, portable anti-aircraft guns, portable anti-tank guns, recoilless rifles, portable launchers of anti-aircraft missile systems, and mortars of diameters of less than 100 mm), which are designed for use by several persons serving as a unit. Ammunition and explosives also form an integral part of small arms and light weapons used in armed conflicts.

Although the arms trafficking is widespread in regions of political unrest, it is not limited to such areas, and for example, in South Asia, an estimated 63 million guns have been trafficked into India and Pakistan. The suppression of gunrunning is one of the areas of increasing interest in the context of international law.

Examples of past and current gunrunning include:

Mexican drug cartel gun imports;

Iran-Contra episode;

Irish Republican Army gun imports;

American "Fast and Furious" gun push into Mexico;

Chechnya illegal gun imports from Turkey.

In the United States, the ironic term "Iron Pipeline" is sometimes used to describe IH 95, on the East Coast, and its connecting side roads to other highways, is a corridor for arms trafficking into New York City area.

The total value of the global arms market is estimated around $800 billion a year, with around $10 billion attributed to pistols, rifles, and bullets. The total illegal arms trade is harder to estimate, but the illicit small arms market has been estimated at 20–30% of the total global arms trade.

One of the most high-profile gun running acts, or "gun walking" the scandals, occurred during President Obama's administration, consisted in a large amount of guns, moved illegally to the drug lords of Mexico.

"Gun walking", or "Letting guns walk", was a tactic of the Arizona Field Office of the United States Bureau of Alcohol, Tobacco, Firearms and Explosives, (ATFE), which ran a series of "sting" operations between 2009 and 2011 in the Tucson and Phoenix areas .where the ATFE "purposely allowed licensed gun dealers to sell weapons to illegal "straw buyers", hoping to track the guns down to Mexican drug cartel leaders and arrest them. These operations were done under the umbrella of a federal code named "Gun runner", a project intended to stem the flow of firearms into Mexico, by interdicting straw purchasers and gun traffickers within the United States.

The Jacob Chambers Case began in October 2009 and eventually became known in February 2010 as the ATF's "Operation Fast and Furious" after agents discovered that Jacob Chambers and the other suspects under investigation, were not gun runners and just belonged to a car club. The goal of allowing these purchases was to continue to track the firearms as they were transferred to higher-level traffickers and key figures in the cartels, with the expectation that this would lead to their arrests and the dismantling of the cartel, however, in this process one border patrol member was murdered with a weapon traced to the ATF sting.

As a result of a dispute over the ATF questionable tactics, the Justice Department was asked to release all the documents related to the Operation Fast and Furious scandal, and the US Attorney General, Eric Holder became the first sitting member of the US Cabinet to be held in contempt of the Congress on June 28, 2012. Earlier that month, President Barack Obama had invoked executive privilege, refusing to allow the Congress to see certain documents.

ATF "gun-walking" operations were, partially, in a direct response to longstanding criticism of the bureau for focusing on relatively minor gun violations while failing to target the high-level gun smuggling figures. U.S. firearms laws, which currently govern the possession and transfer of firearms, will provide penalties for their violation.

Gun trafficking, although not clearly defined by US statutes, essentially refers to the movement of firearms. That may occur in a setting in which the firearms migrate from legal, to some of the illegal markets in innocuous ways.

The ATF initiated several sting operations between 2007 and 2014, unable to put any kind of dent into the illegal international gun trade on either side of the border between USA and Mexico.

Another, smaller incident, occurred in 2007 under the same ATF Phoenix field division's supervision. The Fidel Hernandez case began when the ATF identified Mexican suspects who bought weapons from a Phoenix gun shop, over a span of several months. The probe ultimately involved some 200 guns, a dozen of which were later lost in Mexico. On September 27, 2007, ATF agents saw the original suspects buying weapons at the same store and followed them toward the Mexican border. The ATF informed the Mexican government when the suspects successfully crossed the border, but Mexican law enforcement agents were unable to track them down.

Less than two weeks later, on October 6, William Newell, then ATF's Special Agent in Charge (SAC) of the Phoenix field division, shut down the operation at the behest of William Hoover, ATF's assistant director for the office of field operations.

No charges were filed. Newell, who was Phoenix ATF SAC from June 2006 to May 2011, would later play a major role in the Operation Fast and Furious, which remained out of the reach of the congressional investigations, in an obvious attempt to protect from any liability the Attorney General.

About 2,000 firearms were smuggled into Mexico by straw buyers, under the watchful eyes of the ATF, during the Fast and Furious Operation. These firearms included AK-47, Barrett .50 caliber sniper rifles, .38 caliber revolvers, and Glock 57 pistols. As of October 20, 2011, 389 guns had been recovered in the USA, and 276 had been recovered in Mexico. The rest remained on the streets, floating in the criminal environment. As of February 2012, the total number of recovered firearms was only 710.

Most of the guns went to the Sinaloa Cartel, while others did make their way to "El Teo" and "La Familia" gangs.

When the authorities use illegal methods to entrap offenders in criminal matters, that is similar to the prohibited procedure, which is defined as the "fruit of the poisoned tree", and anything resulting from such actions is not acceptable in a court at law. One would think that the federal government would take advantage of the counsel they may access from the armies of attorneys they keep on the federal payroll. If that is not the case, what comes next?

Is that just a continuation of "business as usual"?

Most likely, that is an indication of our modern world's crass inability to set valid priorities, when it comes to public safety and justice.

That's why it would be absolutely essential to eliminate completely the criminal element's influence on the US legitimate business through consistent law enforcement methods.

The application of drastic punishment measures, for all crimes committed with a firearm, would be a start.

Applying swiftly the death penalty certainly would deter the proliferation of violent crimes, and it would provide the basis for the much needed reconsideration of the judicial process. That certainly would eliminate hardened criminals, instead of just warehousing them, at taxpayers' expense. Keeping one criminal in jails, is just as costly as sending someone to college.

SURVIVING AN ACTIVE SHOOTER

In 2007, a gunman murdered 32 people on the Virginia Tech campus, marking one of the deadliest such crimes in the USA. Some of the intended victims survived, because they emulate some of those who knew what to do. A large number of students got out of that carnage by jumping out from the windows, while others did manage to barricade locked the entry doors into their classrooms.

Making correct decisions, at the proper moment, you could insure your survival, and that of other people with you. The odds that you would be caught in a situation, in which an active shooter dishes mayhem, are quite low. In an FBI study made in 2016, it was found that in the US there are, on the average, there are ten mass shooting per year. The same study suggests that nowhere one can consider himself or herself, safe. There were mass shootings in 45 states of the 50 US sates and commonwealths.

Knowing what to do in such situations may improve your odd of survival considerably:

Identify all the secondary exits, **first time you enter a building;**

Run away, **as soon as an "active shooter" situation occurs;**

React immediately, **when you first hear anything resembling gun fire;**

If the shooter is within your sight, **still run out as fast as you can;**

Lock or barricade a door to prevent shooter's access and do not open it even if someone on the outside yells "Police, open up!";

Once locked in a room, turn the lights off, and use all the furniture inside to your advantage;

Instruct the people with you to turn off cell phones and ask them to remain silent;

Dial 911 only when the noises from the active shooter die down;

If the door cannot be locked, or you do not have the strength to do it, or if there is no heavy furniture, to barricade the door, keep the door from opening using your body. Do not place your back or your shoulder against the door, because the shooter may fire his guns through the door. Instead, lie down on the floor, and keep the door from opening, with your feet. If the gunman shoots, the bullets would fly way above you.

If the door opens outside and you can't lock it shut, use a belt or anything similar, to prevent the door from getting open, while you hold it from outside the door frame, away from possible bullet trajectories.

If neither running away nor denying entry inside the room is possible, you'll have to fight for your survival, as effectively as you could. That includes "fighting dirty". Use anything you can, including any means to neutralizing the shooter, such as throwing salt, sand or anything else in the gunman's eyes, reaching to poke his eyes out, hit him in the head with something heavy, like a fire extinguisher. Discharging a fire extinguisher in the gunman's face can be extremely effective. If you have to fight the shooter, attack him from the side or from the back, using anything you may grab, such as silverware, scissors, or even trash cans. If you get into a close-quarter fight, grab the barrel of the shooter's gun and turn it away from you. If that is a handgun, and you twist it violently, away from you, it may be possible to break the shooter's hand, thus disarming him. Never ever get resigned to the idea that you can't do anything to save your life!

Even if your physical strength is minimal, fighting with all your fibers of your body, may surprise the shooter, and you may find a way to survive. Never fight "gentlemanly".

If there are other people nearby, yell that you got a grip on the shooter's gun, and ask for immediate help. More people would come to help you, better your chances to overcome the shooter.

Of course, a handgun in your hand would even the odds, even if you will be found to possess it illegally, or in a gun-free zone.

Keep in mind that almost all public places have fire exits, or secondary escape doors. In a restaurant they may be in the back of the kitchen, where the people working there may be a deterrent to the actions of an "active shooter".

Playing dead rarely proves to be a good option. Many mass-shooters have been observed to shoot people lying still on the floor, in order to confirm that they were dead.

Statistically, the best course of action that insures the best rate of survival in cases of active shooters indoor, is to get away from that danger zone, as fast as you can, as far as possible.

EPILOGUE

The author attempted to present a comprehensive image of the firearm proliferation in the USA, both under the legal means, and for their use by the criminal element endangering this country's public safety.

The short analysis texts were intended to provide a look into the "anatomy" of few prevalent types of crimes, where some victims were able to turn the tables around, by getting to defend themselves and their property with guns. In such cases most all victims survived. In some other cases, like in the horrible school shootings, the innocent victims did not have a chance.

In the United States, gun laws are found in several federal statutes, enforced by the Bureau of Alcohol, Tobacco, Firearms and Explosives, (ATFE). The right to keep and bear arms is protected by the Second Amendment to the USA Constitution, and almost all state constitutions also guarantee this right. There is some variance across the country as how both federal and state laws apply to firearm possession and ownership. The times we live in today, offer some complex situations that no previous generation ever experienced, and in spite of all the technological advances, our lives did not get better. We still have to work, to get a roof over our heads and meals on our tables. The today's criminals have sophisticated methods to steal and to hurt others, and we all have to be ready to escape safely unforeseen dangers, everywhere. The law enforcement people can't be everywhere, so we have to be mature enough to be able defend ourselves. The God's laws, the US Constitution, and common sense, dictate that we do that, or else we may end up as numbers in statistical reports.

The only advantage we have, over previous generations is the availability of means to stand up against the criminal element. We have a large variety of means to insure our safety and survival. We may get the necessary training to handle guns, similarly to any good insurance policy, in the hope that we will never need to use it, knowing that it is infinitely better to have it, than to need it.

As most survival experts suggest, there are only three ways to act and prepare for handling emergencies:

Situational awareness, means that you need to know in detail what's around you, who may be a threat, and what exits you may have in case circumstances force you to act in your own defense;

Preparedness, means that you got the training necessary to be able to properly handle a situation that may requires the use of a firearm, and to know when to use it, and when not;

Negotiation savvy, means that you are mature enough, to be able to avoid confrontations, and to talk your way out violence. The oriental notion of "peaceful warrior" was never more apt to synthesize the core principles of survival in a world full of criminal violence, and disregard for human life.

Unfortunately, the firearms are an integral part of that.

The controversial positions taken by various media outlets, and a certain group of politicians, regarding gun control, versus those who support the constitutional mandates immortalized by our Founding Fathers, are quite indicative of the lack of any unitary thinking of our citizenry. We were never so deeply divided before in our way of thinking, as today.

Yet both factions those who propose draconic gun control measures, and those that oppose them, do have some valid points, which this small booklet tries to reveal from various perspectives.

The idea that armed security makes people less safe, is a total fallacy that our mass media spreads at nauseam.

Another aspect of this controversy is the thesis that the US Constitution entitles everyone to obtain and bear arms. Some people argue quite unreasonably, that the Constitution does not place any kind of limits on the application of its amendments. Such people argue that no one can find a single mention in the USA Constitution, about people with disabling mental diseases, felons or criminals, since all the citizens are equal under the law. That is a deadly fallacy which did prove often that there is a need to impose some specific limits, in certain areas of law application.

The Congress, as the nation's legislative body, has the duty to see that any wide application of the people's civil rights would not result in harm to anyone. The conclusion that out of some 15 Congressional Acts which do regulate firearms, ever since 1930s, none of them was able to stop the carnage caused by people with guns is valid.

On the other hand, the argument that automobiles in USA do cause much more deaths than guns, over 40,000, and consequently, they have to be all banned, is an artificial one.

Today's politicians seem not to care if their laws work or not. All they want is to pass more laws to limit the rights of the law-abiding citizens to obtain and bear arms. What they miss is to find out that no matter what kind of laws the Congress promulgates, the criminal would never respect any of them.

That illustrates the need to focus on criminal's control and not on gun control. Aside from any other legal points, one has to be aware of the fact that no one act can insure morality, or the correct application of the law, by state, or federal agencies. There will always be some cases in which the criminal element gets to operate "under the radar", or uses unforeseen loopholes in the text of the law, thanks to starving young attorneys. The most prevalent opinions about gun control, vis-à-vis law enforcement, regard the fault of the justice system, which was converted to a thriving "litigation industry", where ineffective judges place the citizenry at risk, through light sentences, which always favor the criminals.

That is a situation that needs urgent reconsideration!

Certain persons are expressly prohibited from obtaining a firearm if:

They have been convicted of a felony, or any other crime for which they could have been sentenced to more than one year in prison, or are under indictment for such acts;

They are fugitives from justice;

They have been convicted of a misdemeanor crime of domestic violence;

They are an unlawful user of, or addicted to, controlled substances, including marijuana;

They have been adjudicated mentally defective;

They have been discharged from the US Armed Forces under dishonorable conditions;

They have renounced their United States citizenship;

The carrying of weapons, either in open or concealed fashion, is regulated by the states, and these laws have changed rapidly over the past decade. As of 2016, most states grant licenses to carry handguns on an individual basis to qualified applicants. A few states leave the issuance of carry permits to the discretion of issuing authorities, while eleven states allow for the carrying of firearms in a concealed form without a permit. Twenty-six states allow for open carrying of handguns without a permit while, in general, twenty states require a permit to do so, and only four states plus Washington, DC ban open-carry of handguns. There have been legal challenges to concealed-carry laws, with different rulings as to their constitutional validity.

The author pays attention to the most vulnerable segment s of our population, women, children and the senior citizens, concluding that the presence of guns in the hands of trained law-abiding citizens deters the crime, in spite what the gun-banning advocates sustain.

Thee dictum that: "It is infinitely better to have a good guy with a gun, on your side, when confronted by a bad guy with a gun", holds much more truth than the idea that you should wait for the arrival of police. Police cannot be every-where, and the criminals do know that, and will take full advantage of it. It is infinitely better to be prepared even for the most illogical situations, to avoid becoming a victim. Sometimes, your gun may not be the answer.

But being educated and trained in the proper use of guns, under various state formulas regarding lawful carry of concealed or open carry, is not any kind of guarantee for your survival in a confrontational situation in which an active shooter is involved.

That's why you need to apply the oriental principles of a "peaceful warrior", who prefers to abstain from harming anyone needlessly. That's why is imperative to know exactly when to use deadly force, and when not to do it.

The following table is meant to offer a synopsis of the general regulations that apply to firearm possession and in terms of minimum age of use:

Firearm use	Age	Carrying
Firearm collectors	21	No carry
Sport shooting	18	Transport only
Hunting	18	Transport only
Professionals, guards	18	Concealed carry
Self-defense	21	Concealed carry

The age limit for sport shooting and for hunting is 16, in certain cases.

Normally, there is very little uniformity in the legal requirements to obtain firearm licenses, with the states that have the most prohibiting regulations, being also the states having the highest level of crime. The current national crime statistics, in many states, indicate a constant decrease in assaults, robberies, and property crimes, since the licensing process to obtain permits to carry, was streamlined in most states. Obviously, the criminal element avoids places where some intended victim may shoot back.

Criminals do not always mug, steal or murder their victims using guns. Recent examples collected from major metropolitan areas prove that many felons use successfully hammers, baseball bats, automobiles, pots and pans, and power tools, to do their dirty deeds.

When you hear about such circumstances, you may, naturally ask what tour odds would be to survive an attack, with a hammer or a baseball bat. If you carry a concealed gun, I would say 100%. If not, only God knows.

If the criminal has the surprise element on his or her side, no one could ascertain the outcome. That's why it is much better to get into a controlled reaction, based on some of the basic defensive techniques you may have been exposed to earlier in your life.

The classic notion expressed by "safety in numbers", especially if you are at risk, as a woman, or a senior citizen, would indicate that it is much better not to do anything alone. Go shopping, to movies, etc. with a group of friends, who if not for anything else, may intimidate the bad guys.

Unfortunately, during the years of the first decade of our 21st century, the frequency of mass shootings increased to an average of some ten such murderous events, almost in all 50 states and commonwealths of the USA.

No one can prepare you to use the best procedures to be able to survive, however, a logical approach would dictate to run away. It is a known fact that no one can outran bullets, but, at the same time, it is awfully hard to hit a moving target.

And that goes for "active shooters", who use at times, a tremendous fire power. The conclusions of this author, is that what we need, is not gun control, but criminals control, as the only logical process capable to minimize the effects of crime upon law-abiding citizens. Only the individuals who hate the American traditions would be dead set to enact universal gun controls of the type the Nazis or other tyrants used.

Our Founding Fathers had good reasons to draft and enact the Second Amendment to the Constitution, to prevent the possibility of hijacking the qualified will of "We the People", by instituting a tyranny.

ABOUT THE AUTHOR

Julian Chitta, a retired electrical engineer, a former US Merchant Marine Officer, a Captain, who is also an avid hunter and fisherman in Texas, has formed an opinion on most all aspects of firearm ownership, through research

He is convinced that the acts of the Congress, meant to regulate firearms, have been originated by good intentions, but not long after adoption they ran into some unanticipated negative consequences.

That gives the impression that the political and legal minds are more concerned with the criminals' comfort than with the welfare of law-abiding taxpayers.

He studied all the 15 sets of acts, currently in force, which deal with firearm regulations, and came to the only logical conclusion, that what the United States need, is not gun control, but "criminal control".

This present booklet tries to examine some of the most prevalent aspects relate to firearm ownership and use.

It cannot answer any legal questions, since the author is not an attorney, but it would prime the reader to enhance his or her correct understanding of principal practices that relate to gun use, in view of current regulations, at state and federal level, about concealed carry, and open carry. Some of the states' mutually agreed regulations are also shown, so that a gun owner may know where the reciprocity rules apply.

During his research he came across several public figures who oppose law-abiding citizen's right to own and use firearms, like Rosie O'Donnell, Nancy Pelosi, and Maxine Watters, all of whom employ personal, armed guards, but oppose the idea of you having the same degree of security, for your own person, and for your possessions.

In this author's opinion, that denotes a questionable level of intelligence, and a high degree of ignorance in matters of reality.

That's hypocrisy at its best!

No matter how you look at the issue of gun control, you have to realize that no full measure can satisfy all circumstances, as the central idea of this booklet is the fact that what America needs is not "gun control", but "crime control", and that would call for a concentrated effort from the part of the legislators to institute some real draconic sentences to criminals using guns. But that would run against the practices used in our litigation industry, where most attorneys and judges make their living from taxpayers' money dished generously to "defend" criminals.

The jurisprudence concept of preferring to allow a criminal to escape just punishment, instead of sentencing an innocent person, only holds this much water. Frequently innocent people end up with heavy sentences, while some notorious criminals get back on the street with just a slap on the wrist.

Is that how the justice system is meant to function?

The USA was never meant to be a popular democracy, but a constitutional republic, where the rule of the law reigns supreme, but the law is what the judges say it is.

During the last few decades the American public got to know a new type of legal professional, the activist judge. Such a judge, regardless if elected or appointed, rules from the bench like a small dictator, turning the statutes inside out in order to justify his own decisions. Sometime they will swing from case law to statutory law, just to satisfy the attorneys practicing in that court.

The adversarial court proceedings resemble a prize fight. The two attorneys, representing their clients punch each other, as hard as they can, in front of the judge. The judge decides which blows are admissible and which ones are under the belt. The winner gets the money, while that lawyer gets rewarded with 33% to 5o% of the fight's purse.

Many times, usually in criminal cases, the fight is between the alleged criminal and the state. Depending of the skills of the attorneys, the criminals often are able to escape any punishment, returning back to their stomping grounds. In cases in which the defendants either win or lose, the taxpayers would pay all the bills especially the attorneys' fees.

Hence the notion of "litigation industry", which seems to be a far cry from what our Founding Fathers envisioned when they did sign the Declaration of Independence, on July 4th, 1776.

As a matter of fact, many of them wanted to outlaw in the United States of America the British custom of "barrister" for any courtroom lawyers. Up to that point, all the civil litigations were supposed to be solved by an impartial judge, selected from the local people based on education, wisdom and dedication to fair and rapid disposition of all cases brought to court. Compare that to years and years of waiting for justice, needed today!

HALL OF FAME

Or rather the "Hall of Shame", shows the most vociferous advocates of gun control, which in their delusional minds drive to invalidate the Second Amendment, so that the law-abiding citizens would be totally deprived of the right to own and use any firearms.

Here they are, in the order of the intensity of their opposition to the Second Amendment of the US Constitution: Hillary Clinton, Rosie O'Donnell, Nancy Pelosi, and Maxine Waters.

Please note that all four of them employ armed guards to insure their security, while advocating the idea that you do not have the right, to enjoy the same level of safety.

They regard the American voters as a bunch of "red necks" who stick to their Bibles, guns, and pickup trucks and they believe that all of them belong in a "basket of deplorable people".

No wonder that only mentally challenged people would vote for them. After the administration of Barack Hussein Obama II, the new Republican Congress is like a breath of fresh air, with the renewed hope for maintaining all the constitutional guarantees for the American people.

Luckily, most voters can separate the chaff from wheat, and when they'll get into the voting booth, they will know exactly how to select the truth, instead of the politicians' toxic lies.

America always overcomes its temporary setbacks!

POST SCRIPTUM

While collecting data for this book, the author came across a lot of statistical information which proved that, during the last five decades, illegal immigration presented a serious threat to our way of living.

Illegal aliens do not integrate into our society, bring in all sort of contagious disease, and frequently engage in criminal activities. This type of situation increases the costs of the administration of local or state governments' work, while unrealistic politicians protect the law breakers, by instituting "sanctuary" zones. This is not the only period in our history when the issue of immigration was "hot". At the turn of the century a massive wave of new immigrants settled here, however, some of them were turned back, for reasons that had to do primarily with health issues. Aside from that, they had to go through a specific immigration process, which entitled them to integrate fully into the American way of life. Today's immigrants fail to do the same, preferring to remain in isolated enclaves, which copy the situation in their old countries of origin. Consequently there you could find entire sections of our larger cities, where people cannot speak any English. Marginalized, such people frequently engage in criminal activities.

The observation that many illegal immigrants have a marked predilection for criminal activities is not just an incorrect political position, as the leftist media would push you to believe. That is a fact which underlines some of the today's negative realities.

In 1907, Theodore Roosevelt, while on his electoral train trips, made several speeches that synthesized the contemporary opinions regarding the immigration phenomena:

"In the first place we should insist that if the immigrant who comes here **in good faith** becomes an American and he **assimilates** himself to us, he shall be treated on an **exact equality** with every-one else, for it is an outrage to discriminate against any such man because of creed, or birthplace, or origin. But this **is predicated upon the person's becoming in every facet an American**, and nothing but an American. There can be no divided allegiance here. Any man who says that he is an American, but something else also, isn't an American at all. We have room for one flag, **the American flag**. We have room for one language here, and that is the **English language**, and we have room for but one sole loyalty, and that is the **loyalty to the American people.**"

Seeing illegal immigrants, protesting against something that they perceive as the unfairness of the US laws, while waiving some foreign flags, you cannot abstain from remembering what that US president believed in. The immigrants of his period worked to become Americans, body and soul. The today's immigrants do not ever consider integrating fully into our society, content to make their money here and eventually, to return to the old country.

Is that a normal sign of our times, or just an anomaly?

www.ingramcontent.com/pod-product-compliance
Lightning Source LLC
Chambersburg PA
CBHW052302220526
45471CB00001B/458